Sergey's
HTML5
& CSS3
Quick Reference

By Sergey Mavrody, MFA
Belisso Corporation
2010

Sergey's HTML5 & CSS3 Quick Reference

Author Sergey Mavrody, MFA

Editor Nika Mavrody

Find us on the World Wide Web for updates: http://html5.belisso.com
Or contact Sergey directly at belissohtml5@gmail.com

Belisso Corporation

Notice of Rights

Notice of Liability

About the Author

Sergey Mavrody has been working with web technologies since the mid-nineties, focusing on UI design and development, creative direction, information architecture, interactive media, and enterprise applications with rich data visualization and advanced user interface components. Sergey holds two master's degrees. He is also a visual artist and educator with many years experience teaching as professor at the School of the Art Institute of Chicago.

Dedication

For Natasha and Nika. I love you!

For people who read books.

Table of Contents

1. Intro to HTML5

Overview

About this book

HTML and CSS are the most essential and fundamental web languages: they provide the foundation for the vast majority of web sites and web applications. HTML5 is on track to become the future of the web, offering simple plug-in free Rich Internet Application capabilities, easier development, and enhanced user experience.

Today you can find a wealth of HTML5 information on the web including references, tutorials and tips. There are also a few very good books available which concentrate on certain HTMl5 features. However there is always a need for a relatively concise summary of all that information in one handy reference-style book.

This book is an essential technical dictionary for professional web designers and developers, conveniently summarizing over 3000 pages of (X)HTML5 and CSS3 specifications and covering the most common and fundamental concepts and specs, including tags, attributes, values, objects, properties, methods, events, and APIs.

Topics include:

- Introduction to HTML5
- HTML5 and XTML5 syntax rules
- Document semantic structure
- Complete reference to HTML5 Elements and Attributes including Web Forms 2.0
- Global attributes and events
- A complete summary of CSS3 properties
- HTML5 APIs, including Canvas, SVG, Video, Audio, Web Workers, Web Sockets, Microdata, Geolocation, Web Storage and more.

The author's goal was to create a one-stop resource reference source which is comprehensive but still concise, simple, easy-to-read, and structured.

What is HTML?

The well-known acronym 'HTML' stands for HyperText Markup Language. It is the primary markup language for the world wide web, capable of creating web documents by specifying content structure including headings, paragraphs, tables, footers and other elements.

The HTML markup also typically utilizes CSS (Cascading Style Sheets) to describe the visual appearance of content. CSS enables the separation of document HTML content from document visual presentation, such as the layout, colors, and fonts.

HTML allows for the creation of interactive forms as well as the embedding of images, video, audio and other objects. HTML code can embed scripts, such as JavaScript, which contribute to dynamic behavior of web pages.

Major HTML versions

- The first HTML document called "HTML Tags", was published by Berners-Lee in 1991.

- HTML 4.0 was published as a World Wide Web Consortium (W3C) recommendation in 1997, offering three variations: transitional, strict, and frameset.

- XHTML 1.0, a more restrictive subset of HTML markup, was published in 2000-2002. It conforms to XML syntax requirements.

- XHTML 2.0 working drafts were released in 2002-2006. The proposed standard attempted to make a more radical break from the past versions, but sacrificed a backward compatibility. Later the W3C decided to halt any further development of the draft into a standard, in favor of more flexible HTML5 standard.

- HTML5 first public draft was released by the W3C in 2008.

- XHTML5 is under development since 2009.

HTML5

The HTML5 development began in 2004 by an informal group of experts from Apple Computer, the Mozilla Foundation, and Opera Software forming the WHATWG group (Web Hypertext Application Technology Working Group). The WHATWG HTML5 specification was eventually adopted by the World Wide Web Consortium (W3C) in 2007.

- The HTML5 markup is more backward compatible with HTML 4 and XHTML 1.0 vs. XHTML 2.0.

- HTML5 introduces many new elements, including semantic replacements for generic HTML elements. For instance new layout elements, such as `<header>`, `<footer>`, `<section>`, `<nav>`, `<article>` were created. Many HTML 4 elements were retired (deprecated).

- HTML5 also introduces many additional plugin-free capabilities such as standardized video and audio interface, raster imaging, local database, offline mode, more efficient multi-threaded JavaScript, Cross Document Messaging and more.

XHTML5

XHTML5 is the XML serialization of HTML5. XHTML5 document is served with an XML MIME type, e.g. `application/xhtml+xml`. Also XHTML5 requires stricter well-formed syntax. In XHTML5 document the HTML5 document type declaration is optional and may be omitted. XHTML5 may be utilized to extend HTML5 to some XML-based technologies such as *SVG* and *MathML*.

CSS3

The new version of CSS is introduced and approved in modules which allow for more flexibility to be released. New features of CSS3 are quite extensive:

- Selectors offer a much more specific way of selecting elements, including matching on attributes and attribute values, structural pseudo-classes, target pseudo-class to style only elements that are targeted in the URL, a checked pseudo-class to style any element that is checked such as radio or checkbox elements
- Text Effects and Layout, including hyphenation, 'whitespace', and justification of text
- Paged Media and Generated Content, supporting more options in paged media, such as running headers, footers, page numbering, footnotes and cross-references
- Multi-Column Layout properties allow for multiple column layouts
- First-Letter and First-Line pseudo-classes
- Ruby module offers ability to add small annotations on top or next to words, used in Asian scripts

Why use HTML5?

- Backward compatibility: HTML5 is wrapping up all previous doctypes
- Simpler Syntax: improved semantics, more productive coding and smaller document size
- New elements and attributes make design and development more flexible
- Plugin-free video and audio and timed media playback
- Smart Web Forms 2.0 functionality (HTML5 Supersedes Web Forms 2.0)
- Ability to use in-line *SVG* and *MathML* in with `text/html` MIME type
- New plugin-free scripting APIs (application programming interfaces), including:
  - Canvas element 2D graphics
  - Cross-document messaging
  - Document editing
  - Drag-and-drop
  - Geolocation
  - Local offline storage and local SQL Database
  - MIME type and protocol handler registration
  - Microdata
- The bottom line: easier development and enhanced user experience

Who this book is for

This diagram below was inspired by Jesse Garrett's diagram The Elements of User Experience. This diagram is centred around typical web application development cycle and various roles involved, most of which would benefit from HTML5 and CSS3 knowledge and/or skills.

Anyone who is familiar with HTML and CSS and who is interested in web site/web application development, design and user experience issues would benefit from reading this book.

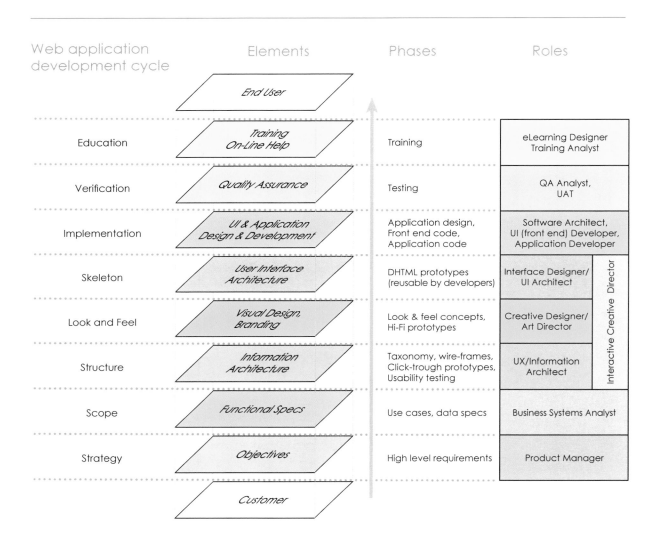

2. HTML Syntax

HTML document

Basics

Generally, HTML document represents a standalone HTML file.

- HTML document is a code assembled of *elements* and text.
- Elements are basic HTML building blocks, represented by HTML tags.
- Elements form a hierarchical nested structure.

Elements and Tags

Each element is denoted by an opening tag, *in this example:* `<title>`, and a corresponding closing tag `</title>`. In some cases a closing tag is not required.

The difference between an element and a tag is that an *element* is a conceptual representation of HTML tag, which can also include its attributes and child tags.

Tag nesting

- Tag is denoted by the less than (<) and greater than (>) inequality signs.
- Nested tag pairs have to be completely within each other, without overlapping with another pair.

```
<!DOCTYPE html>

<html>

<head>
<title>HTML5 Reference</title>

<!-- This is a comment. It does not
render in browser -->

</head>
        <body>

        <h1>Overview</h1>

        <p>The well-known acronym
HTML stands for HyperText Markup
Language.</p>

        </body>

</html>
```

```
The <b><em>wrong</b></em> nesting

The <b><em>correct</em></b> nesting
```

Void Elements

Void element has only an opening tag and therefore it can not have any content. A terminating slash may optionally be inserted at the end of the element's tag, immediately before the closing greater-than sign. For a non-void element the terminating slash is illegal.

```
<!--Void elements:-->

<img src=logo.gif><br />

<input type=text>
```

Attributes

An element *in this example:* **input** can have multiple attributes **type, autofocus, name.**

```
<input type=text autofocus
name='first name'>
```

- An attribute is a property of an element.
- Attributes are placed inside the opening tag.
- The tag name and attribute are both separated by white space.
- An attribute is assembled with a name **type** and a value **text**, separated by the equal (=) sign.
- No duplicate attributes allowed within a tag.
- HTML5 attribute value can remain un-quoted if it doesn't contain spaces, quotation marks or inequality signs **type=text**. Otherwise, an attribute value has to be quoted using either single or double quotes **'first name'**.

Boolean attribute

A boolean attribute is a property that represents either a false or true value.

- The absence of a boolean attribute implies a value of "false".

```
<!--boolean value is false:
the field is NOT disabled-->

<input>
```

- The presence of a boolean attribute implies that the value of the attribute is "true".
- Boolean attribute may take the name of the attribute itself as a value **<input disabled=disabled>**.
- In a *polyglot* HTML/XHTML document, a boolean attribute with a true value is coded with a quoted value that matches the attribute name **<input disabled="disabled">**.

```
<!--boolean value is true-->

<input disabled=disabled>

<input disabled="disabled">

<input disabled="">

<input disabled>
```

- In a non-polyglot HTML document the value can be excluded **<input disabled>**.

XHTML5

Polyglot HTML document

A polyglot HTML document is a document that is valid in both *HTML* and *XHTML*.

- A polyglot HTML document obeys both HTML and XHTML syntax rules by using a common subset of both the HTML and XHTML syntax.

- A polyglot document can serve as either HTML or XHTML, depending on browser support and *MIME type*.

- The choice of HTML vs. Polyglot syntax is dependent upon the project objectives, browser support, and other factors.

```
<!--HTML4, HTML5 syntax-->
<input disabled>
<input disabled=disabled>

<!--XHTML 1.0 syntax-->
<input disabled="disabled" />

<!--HTML4, HTML5, XHTML 1.0
conforming Polyglot syntax-->
<input disabled="disabled" />
```

XHTML5 defined

A polyglot HTML5 code essentially becomes an *XHTML5* document if it is served with the XML MIME type [`application/xhtml+xml`]. In a nutshell the HTML5 polyglot document is:

- HTML5 DOCTYPE/namespace. HTML5 no longer needs to refer to a Document Type Definition since HTML5 is no longer formally based on SGML. However, the DOCTYPE is needed for backward compatibility.

- XHTML well-formed syntax

A polyglot document can serve as either HTML or XHTML, depending on browser support and MIME type. A polyglot HTML5 code essentially becomes an XHTML5 document if it is served with the XML MIME type: `application/xhtml+xml` . In a nutshell the XHTML5 document is:

- XML declaration `<?xml version="1.0" encoding="UTF-8"?>` is not required if the default UTF-8 encoding is used.

- HTML DOCTYPE: The `<!DOCTYPE html>` declaration is optional, but it may be used if the document is intended to be a polyglot document that may be served as both HTML or XHTML.

- XHTML well-formed syntax

- XML MIME type: application/xhtml+xml. This MIME declaration is not visible in the source code, but it appears in the HTTP Content-Type header when it's configured on the server. Of course, the XML MIME type is not yet supported by the current version Internet Explorer though IE can render XHTML documents.

- Default XHTML namespace: `<html xmlns="http://www.w3.org/1999/xhtml">`

- Secondary SVG, MathML, Xlink, etc. namespace: To me, this is like a test: if you don't have a need for these namespaces in your document, then using XHTML is overkill. But, essentially, the choice between HTML5 and XHTML5 boils down to the choice of a media type.

Finally, the basic XHTML5 document would look like this:

The XML declaration `<?xml version="1.0" encoding="UTF-8"?>` is not required if the default UTF-8 encoding is used: an XHTML5 validator would not mind if it is omitted.

However, it is strongly recommended to configure the encoding using server HTTP Content-Type header, otherwise this character encoding could be included in the document as part of a meta tag `<meta charset="UTF-8" />`.

This encoding declaration would be needed for a polyglot document so that it's treated as UTF-8 if served as either HTML or XHTML.

The Total Validator Tool - Firefox plugin/desktop app has now the user-selectable option for XHTML5-specific validation.

```
<!DOCTYPE html>

<html xmlns="http://www.
w3.org/1999/xhtml">

<head>

  <title></title>

  <meta charset="UTF-8" />

</head>

<body>

  <svg xmlns="http://www.
w3.org/2000/svg">

    <rect stroke="black" fill="blue"
x="45px" y="45px" width="200px"
height="100px" stroke-width="2" />

  </svg>

</body>

</html>
```

The main advantage of using XHTML5 would be the ability to extend HTML5 to XML-based technologies such as SVG and MathML. Even though SVG and MathML are supported inline by HTML5 specification, browser support is currently limited. The disadvantage is the lack of Internet Explorer support, more verbose code, and error handling. Unless you need that extensibility, HTML5 is the way to go.

Ultimately, the choice between HTML5 and XHTML5 comes down to the choice of a MIME/content type, that determines what type of document you are using. Unlike XHTML1 vs. HTML4, the XHTML5 vs. HTML5 choice of is exclusively dependent upon the choice of the MIME type, rather than the DOCTYPE.

Document Type and Structure

MIME Type

"MIME" stands for Multipurpose Internet Mail Extensions. MIME type is also called an *Internet Media Type* or *Content Type*. It is similar to file extensions identifying a type of information and it requires at least two components: a type, a subtype, and some optional parameters.

```
<!DOCTYPE html>
  <head>
    <title>HTML5</title>
    <link media=screen type=text/css
    href=styles.css rel=stylesheet>
  </head>
    <body></body>
</html>
```

Common MIME Types

Type	Content Type/Subtype code	Description
Application	application/javascript	JavaScript
	application/xhtml+xml	XHTML
Audio	audio/mpeg	MPEG, MP3 audio
	audio/x-ms-wma	Windows Media Audio
	audio/vnd.rn-realaudio	RealAudio
Image	image/gif	GIF image
	image/jpeg	JPEG image
	image/png	Portable Network Graphics
	image/svg+xml	SVG vector graphics
Message	message/http	Message
Text	text/css	Cascading Style Sheets
	text/csv	Comma-separated values
	text/html	HTML
	text/javascript	JavaScript. This type is obsolete, but allowed in HTML 5. It has cross-browser support, unlike **application/javascript**.
	text/plain	Basic Text
	text/xml	Extensible Markup Language
Video	video/mpeg	MPEG-1 video
	video/mp4	MP4 video
	video/quicktime	QuickTime video
	video/x-ms-wmv	Windows Media Video

The majority of media types could be accessed at the IANA site, the Internet Assigned Numbers Authority: **www.iana.org/assignments/media-types**.

Document Object Model (DOM)

A web browser creates a model of HTML document represented by a tree of objects, such elements, attributes, and text. This model is called *Document Object Model*, *DOM*. DOM objects could be manipulated by JavaScript. An object instance of a hierarchical DOM tree called a *node*.

```
<div onclick="document.
getElementById('description').
style.display = 'none';">
Hide Description</div>

<div id=description>Overview</div>
```

In this example button action invokes JavaScript, finding the object ID of the Overview container and hiding the DIV container.

Semantic page structure

(X)HTML5 offers new elements forming semantic structure of a web page.

Element	Typical Content	Typical Parent and	Child Elements
`<header>`	title, logo, banner, Introductory information	Body, Section, Article	Nav, Section
`<nav>`	Primary navigation menu	Body	Section, Nav
`<section>`	Generic page section	Body	Article, Header, Footer, Aside, Nav
`<article>`	Story, subsection, blog post,	Body, Section	Section, Header, Footer
`<aside>`	Sidebar content, tip, quotation	Body	Section, Article
`<footer>`	Footer, summary, copyright info, secondary navigation	Body, Section, Article	Nav, Section

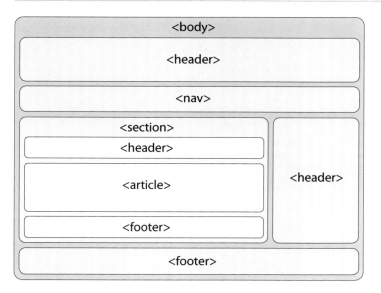

Syntax Summary

General Syntax Rules

Rule	HTML5 syntax	XHTML5 syntax
XML declaration	n/a	not required, if the default UTF-8 encoding is used
		`<?xml version="1.0" encoding="UTF-8"?>`
DOCTYPE	required	not required
MIME type	`text/html`	`application/xhtml+xml`
Case sensitive attributes values	not required	required
White space normalization in attribute values	White space characters are not normalized	White space characters are normalized to single space with some exceptions
Low case attributes	not required	required
Attribute quotes	not required, except when attribute contains spaces or characters: `"  '  ` `  =  <  >`	required
	`<image alt=logo>` `<image alt='company logo'>`	`<image alt="logo" />`
Full boolean attribute	not required, attribute minimization is allowed	required, attribute minimization is illegal
	`<input disabled=disabled>` `<input disabled="disabled">` `<input disabled="">` `<input disabled>`	`<input disabled="disabled" />`
Terminating slash in void elements	not required	required
	` ` or ` ;` `<hr>` or `<hr/>;` `<img>` or `<img />;` `<input>` or `<input />`	` ` `<hr />` `<img />` `<input />`
Element names	case insensitive	case sensitive, lower-case

Rule	HTML5 syntax	XHTML5 syntax
Opening and Closing tags for non-void elements	optional, in some elements, based on certain conditions, see table below	required
Un-escaped Special Characters	Un-escaped ampersands (&) and less than signs (<) are generally permitted within elements and attribute values. Some exceptions apply.	Un-escaped ampersands (&) and 'less than' signs (<) are not permitted within elements and attribute values and must be substituted respectively with & and <

(X)HTML5 void tag syntax

- Void tags has no closing (end) tag: <input> </input>
- HTML5 - terminating slash in void elements is not required: <input>
- XHTML5 - terminating slash in void elements is required: <input />

area	command	img	meta
base	embed	input	param
br	hr	link	source
col			

HTML5 elements with optional tags

- Optional tags are not applicable for XHTML5 document.
- The Condition column indicates the condition when the tag is optional.
  - Usually, **at least one** condition has to be met to allow an omitted tag
  - Some tags have no condition information available at the time of writing

Element	Start Tag	Condition	End Tag	Condition
`<body>` `</body>`	optional	▪ *Body* is empty ▪ Not followed by a *space* character ▪ Not followed by a *comment* tag ▪ Except when *script* or *style* element is next	optional	▪ Not followed by a *comment* tag
`<colgroup>` `</colgroup>`	required	n/a	optional	▪ Not followed by a *space* character

Element	Start Tag	Condition	End Tag	Condition
<dd></dd>	required	n/a	optional	▪ Not followed by a *dt* or *dd* element
<dt></dd>	required	n/a	optional	▪ Not followed by a *dt* or *dd* element ▪ It is the last description term
<head> </head>	optional	▪ *Head* is empty, or ▪ Not followed by another element	optional	▪ Not followed by a *space* character ▪ Not followed by a *comment* element
<html> </html>	optional	▪ Not followed by a *comment* element	optional	▪ Not followed by a *comment* element
<li></li>	required	n/a	optional	▪ Followed by another *li* element ▪ It is the last item within the parent element
<optgroup> </optgroup>	required	n/a	optional	▪ It is the last *optgroup* element ▪ It is the last item within the parent element
<option> </option>	required	n/a	optional	▪ Followed by another *option* element ▪ Followed by an *optgroup* element ▪ It is the last item within the parent element
<p></p>	required	n/a	optional	▪ Followed by these tags: *address, article, aside, blockquote, dir, div, dl, fieldset, footer, form, h1, h2, h3, h4, h5, h6, header, hgroup, hr, menu, nav, ol, p, pre, section, table,* or *ul* ▪ It is the last item within the parent element
<tbody> </tbody>	optional	n/a	optional	▪ Followed by a *tbody* element ▪ Followed by a *tfoot* element ▪ It is the last item within the parent element
<td></td>	required	n/a	optional	▪ Followed by a *td* element ▪ Followed by a *th* element ▪ It is the last item within the parent element

Element	Start Tag	Condition	End Tag	Condition
`<tfoot>` `</tfoot>`	optional	n/a	optional	■ Followed by a *tbody* ■ It is the last item within the parent element
`<th>` `</th>`	required	n/a	optional	■ Followed by a *td* element ■ Followed by a *th* element ■ It is the last item within the parent element
`<thead>` `<thead>`	optional	n/a	optional	■ Followed by a *tbody* ■ Followed by a *tfoot*
`<tr></tr>`	required	n/a	optional	■ Followed by a *tr* element ■ It is the last item within the parent element

Example of a valid HTML5 document omitting optional tags, versus so called *well-formed* XHTML5 document, checked with Total Validator tool:

HTML5

```
<!DOCTYPE html>


   <title>HTML5 document</title>


 <table title=Report>
  <tr>
   <td>1st cell content
   <td>2nd cell content
   <td>3rd cell content

  <tr>
   <td>4th cell content
   <td>5th cell content
   <td>6th cell content

 </table>
```

XHTML5

```
<html xmlns="http://www.
w3.org/1999/xhtml">

<head>
   <title>XHTML5 document</title>
</head>
<body>

 <table title="Report">
  <tr>
   <td>1st cell content</td>
   <td>2nd cell content</td>
   <td>3rd cell content</td>
  </tr>

  <tr>
   <td>4th cell content</td>
   <td>5th cell content</td>
   <td>6th cell content</td>
  </tr>

 </table>

</body>

</html>
```

Elements by Type

Type	Elements			
Root	html			
Metadata	head title	base link	meta style	
Scripting	script	noscript		
Sections	body section element	nav article aside	h1, h2, h3, h4, h5, h6 header	footer address
Grouping	p hr br	pre dialog blockquote	ol ul li	dl dt dd
Inline Semantics	a q cite em strong small mark	dfn abbr time progress meter code var	samp kbd sub sup span i b	bdo ruby rt rp
Edits	ins	del		
Embedded Content	figure img iframe	embed object param	video audio The source	canvas map area
Tabular Data	table caption colgroup	col tbody thead	tfoot tr td	th
Forms	form fieldset label	input button select	datalist optgroup option	textarea output
Interactive Elements	details	command	bb	menu
Miscellaneous Elements	legend	div		

Browser Compatibility Scripting

Due to the fact that HTML5 browser support is inconsistent, JavaScript can be used in order to target specific browser functionality or add missing functionality.

HTML5 compatibility detection

- The most effective tool is *Modernizr*, an open source JavaScript library that detects support for HTML5 and CSS3. The latest version of *Modernizr* library can be downloaded from modernizr.com web site.

```
<!DOCTYPE html>
<html>
<head><title></title>

  <script src="modernizr.min.js"></script>

</head>
```

HTML5 enabling scripts

- HTML5 Modernizr is a detection tool: it does not add missing HTML5 functionality to older browsers, however Modernizr site has a page "HTML5-Cross-browser-Polyfills", which is a collection of useful links for many various solutions of this kind. *Polyfill* is a piece of code or plugin that allows developer to provide a technology browser is missing. Polyfills fill in the gaps to make HTML5 and CSS3 usable today even in older browsers.

3. HTML5 Elements

General Definitions

Chapter Legend & Conventions

- Attributes listed are specific for each tag, otherwise an element supports all global attributes.
- Global attributes are listed in Chapter 4.
- Values in { } brackets are variable placeholders for actual values.
- Values in regular text are actual valid values.
- Elements displayed in gray color are deprecated (obsolete).
- The sample code offered is mostly based on HTML5 syntax, not XHTML5.

Summary of HTML5 Elements

- This section describes all the different types of element that you can use to write an HTML document.
- HTML5 specifications are still in draft mode, and could potentially change.
- The [5] symbol indicates that this is new HTML5 element or attribute.

Tag	Code Example	Description
<!-- -->	<!-- this comment does not render in browser -->	Comment
<!DOCTYPE>	<!DOCTYPE HTML> <html> <head> <title>Title</title> </head> <body>World</body> </html>	Generally, *Document Type Definition* (DTD) specifies language and version of HTML used for the document. In HTML 5 the **<!DOCTYPE>** tag is simplified and it does not require a reference to a DTD. The **<!DOCTYPE>** tag is included for backward compatibility.

Tag	Code Example		Description
`<a>`	`<a href=http://html5.belisso.com>Belisso Publishing</a>`		A hyperlink to another page or an *anchor*
	Attribute	**Value**	**Description**
	charset	{char encoding}	Deprecated in HTML5
	coords	{coordinates}	Deprecated in HTML5
	href	{URL}	Target URL
	hreflang	language_code	Base language of the URL. Use only if the *href* attribute is present
	media	media query	Media type of the target URL. Default value: all. Use only if the *href* attribute is present
	name	{text string}	Deprecated in HTML5
	ping	{URL}	Space-separated list of URL's that gets notified when a user follows the hyperlink. Use only if the *href* attribute is present
	rel	alternate, archives, author, bookmark, external, feed, first, help, index, last, license, next, nofollow, noreferrer, prev, search, sidebar, tag, up	Relationship between the document and the destination URL. The *href* attribute must be present. Accepts multiple values, separated by a space.
`<abbr>`	`<abbr title="United Nations">UN</abbr> is an international organization.`		Abbreviation / acronym. Title attribute may be used to describe the abbreviation.
`<acronym>`			Deprecated in HTML5
`<address>`	`<address>` `Address: 1414 N. Clark ` `Chicago, IL 60610 ` `Ph: 312 285 7867` `</address>`		Address element, renders in italic
`<applet>`			Deprecated in HTML5

Tag	Code Example	Description

`<area>`	`<img src =shapes.gif width=166 height=132 alt=shapes usemap=#shapemap>`
	
	`<map name=shapemap>`
	`<area shape=rect coords=0,0,60,90 href=square.htm alt=square>`
	
	  `<area shape=circle coords=50,25,5  href=circle. htm alt=circle>`
	
	  `<area shape=poly coords=152,572,163,611, 211,610,223,574,193,546, 152,573 href=pentagon.htm alt=pentagon>`
	`</map>`
		Image map area
		
		Image maps are images with clickable areas (sometimes referred to as "hotspots") that usually link to another page.

Attribute	Value	Description
alt	text	Alternate text for the area. This attribute requires the *href* attribute.
coords	Shape *rect*: left,top,right,bottom Shape *circ*: centerx,centery,radius Shape *poly*: x1,y1,x2,y2 ... xn,yn	Clickable area definition: coordinates
href	{URL}	Target URL of the area
hreflang **5**	{language code}	Base language of the target URL. This attribute requires the *href* attribute

media **5**	<u>all</u>, aural, braille, handheld, projection, print, screen, tty, tv, {width}, {height}, {device-width}, {device-height}, {orientation}, {grid} {aspect-ratio}, {device-aspect-ratio}, {color}, {color-index}, {monochrome}, {resolution}, {scan},	Defines the device media type of the target URL. This attribute requires the *href* attribute. Operators **and**, **not** and (**,**) comma could be utilized to combine multiple values. Example:
		
		`<a href=media.html`
		
		`media="screen and (aspect-ratio:16/9)">`
		
		`View Video</a>`

Tag	Code Example	Description
nohref		Not supported in HTML 5.
ping ❺	{URL}	Space delimited list of URL's notified when a user follows the URL. This attribute requires the *href* attribute
rel	Alternate, archives, author, bookmark, contact, external, first, help, icon, index, last, license, next, nofollow, noreferrer, pingback, prefetch, prev, search, stylesheet, sidebar, tag, up	Specifies the relationship between the current document and the target URL. This attribute requires the *href* attribute.
shape	rect, rectangle, circ, circle, poly, polygon	Shape of the area
target	_blank, _parent, _self, _top	Where to open the target URL. *_blank*: new window *_self*: same frame *_parent*: parent frameset *_top*: full body of the window
type ❺	{mime type}	Specifies the Multipurpose Internet Mail Extensions type of the target URL. This attribute requires the *href* attribute.

`<article>` ❺	`<article>`
	`<a href=http://www.wikipedia.com>HTML5</a>Serving as virtual librarians, Wikipedia volunteers tackle your questions on a wide range of subjects.<time pubdate datetime=2009-10-10T19:15-08:00></time>`
	`</article>`
		External content such as a news article or blog excerpt.
		
		The *time* element with *datetime* attribute may be used.

Tag	Code Example	Description

`<aside>` 5	`<article><h1>HTML5</h1>` `<p>HTML5 is being developed as the next major revision of HTML.</p>`
	
	`<aside>` `<p>Generations of HTML:</p>` `<ul>` `    <li>HTML4` `    <li>XHTML1` `    <li>HTML5` `</ul>` `</aside></article>`
		Aside content is additional information that can enhance main content. Examples may include a tip or a list of facts.
		
		 Aside element should not be used for ads, navigation menu, search boxes, or any other unrelated content.

`<audio>` 5	`<audio src=audiofile.mp3 controls autoplay></audio>`	Sound content

Attribute	Value	Description
autoplay	{boolean}	Audio will start playing automatically
controls	{boolean}	Displays Audio controls
preload	{boolean}	Audio will preload at page load, and be ready to play. This attribute will be ignored if *autoplay* is present.
src	{URL}	URL of the audio to play

Tag	Code Example	Description
`<b>`	The `<b>`bold`</b>` text	Bold
`<base>`	`<head>` `<base href=http://www.domain.com target=_blank>` `</head>`	Default URL and default target for all page links.

Attribute	Value	Description
href	{URL}	Target URL of the area
target	_blank, _parent, _self, _top	Where to open the target URL. ■ *_blank*: new window ■ *_self*: same frame ■ *_parent*: parent frameset ■ *_top*: full body of the window

Tag	Code Example	Description
`<basefont>`		Deprecated in HTML5

Tag	Code Example		Description
<bdo>	<bdo dir=rtl> Hebrew text </bdo>		Direction of text display. The *dir* attribute is required.
	Attribute	**Value**	**Description**
	dir	ltr, rtl	Defines direction
<big>			Deprecated in HTML5
<blockquote>			Long quotation
	Attribute	**Value**	**Description**
	cite	{URL}	Target URL of the area
<body>	<html> <head> <title>Page Title</title> </head> <body>page content</body> </html>		Browser rendered page content.
 	<p>John Smith (312) 234-5678</p>		Line break
<button>	<button type=button name=next autofocus>Next Page</button>		Push button
	Attribute	**Value**	**Description**
	autofocus [5]	{boolean}	Sets focus on the button when the page loads.
	disabled	{boolean}	Sets button state to disabled.
	form [5]	{text string}	Specifies which form this button belongs to.
	formaction [5]	{URL}	Specifies where to submit form data. Overrides the form's *action* attribute.
	formenctype [5]	application/x-www-form-urlencoded multipart/form-data text/plain	Specifies how form-data should be encoded before sending it to a server. Overrides the form's *enctype* attribute.
	formmethod [5]	delete, get, post, put	Specifies how to send form-data. Overrides the form's *action* attribute.

Tag	Code Example		Description
	formnovalidate	{boolean}	The form should not be validated when submitted. Overrides the form's *novalidate* attribute.
	formtarget ❺	_blank, _self, _parent, _top	Where to open the target URL. ■ *_blank*: new window ■ *_self*: same frame ■ *_parent*: parent frameset ■ *_top*: full body of the window
	name	{text string}	Unique name for the button
	type	button, reset, submit	Button type
	value	{text string}	An initial button value, which can be changed by a script.
`<canvas>` ❺	`<canvas id=myCanvas height=90 width=90></canvas>`		HTML rendered graphics.

```
<script type=text/javascript>
var canvas=document.
getElementById('graphics');
var ctx=canvas.
getContext('2d');
ctx.fillStyle='#CFEBE2';
ctx.fillRect(0,0,50,80);
</script>
```

Attribute	Value	Description
height	{number} pixels, %	Canvas height
width	pixels	Canvas width

Tag	Code Example	Description

`<caption>`	`<table>`
	`<caption>`Revenue`</caption>`
	`<tr>`
	  `<th>`2009
	  `<th>`2010
	`<tr>`
	  `<td>`$12.6 Billion
	  `<td>`$13.2 Billion
	`</table>`
		Table caption

Revenue

2009	$12.6 Billions
2010	$13.2 Billions

Tag	Description
`<center>`	Deprecated in HTML5

Tag	Code Example		Description
`<cite>`	`<cite>To be or not 2 b?</cite>`		Citation
	Attribute	Value	Description
	cite	{URL}	Source of the citation
`<code>`	`<code>return{find(chars.begin())!=chars.end()}</code>`		Programming code text
`<col>`	`<table>`		Applies attributes to a column

```
<table>
<col span=2 style=background-color:Lavender>
<col style=background-color:MistyRose>
  <tr>
    <td>1st group
    <td>1st group
    <td>2nd group

  <tr>
    <td>1st group
    <td>1st group
    <td>2nd group
</table>
```

1st group	1st group	2nd group
1st group	1st group	2nd group

Attribute	Value	Description
span	{number}	Defines number of columns grouped by the attribute
align	left, right, center, justify, char	Deprecated in HTML5
char	{character}	
charoff	{number}	
valign	top, middle, bottom, baseline	
width	{number} %, pixels	

Tag	Code Example		Description

`<colgroup>`	```<table>```
	
	```<colgroup span=2 style=```
	```"background-color:#CFEBE2">```
	```<tr>```
	``` <th>Year</th>```
	``` <th>Make</th>```
	``` <th>Model</th>```
	```</tr>```
			Group of table columns. The *colgroup* element can only contain *col* element.
			
			Closing tag `</colgroup>` is not required.

Attribute	Value	Description
span	{number}	Defines number of columns grouped by the attribute
align	left, right, center, justify, char	Deprecated in HTML5
char	{character}	
charoff	{number}	
valign	top, middle, bottom, baseline	
width	{percents}, {pixels}	

Tag	Code Example	Description

`<command>` ❺	```<menu>```
	
	```<command type=command```
	```icon=image.png disabled>Home```
	
	```</menu>```
		The `<command>` element defines a command button, such as check box or a button. Requires parent *menu* element. Closing tag `</command>` is not required.

Attribute	Value	Description
checked	{boolean}	Defines if the command (radio or checkbox) is checked.
disabled	{boolean}	Defines if the command is available.
icon	{URL}	URL of an image represents the command
label	{command name}	Name for the command visible to the users
radiogroup	{text string}	Name of the *radiogroup* this command (a radio button) belongs to
title	{text string}	Tool tip
type ❺	checkbox, radio, command	Type of command

Tag	Code Example	Description

<datagrid> [5]

```
<datagrid>

<ol>
<li>Data row 0
<li>Data row 1

<ol style=list-style-type:
alpha>
  <li>Data row 1,0
  <li>Data row 1,1
</ol>

</li>
  <li>Data row 2
</ol>

</datagrid>
```

Currently dropped from HTML5 specs.

Interactive tree, list or data table. Data is structured as zero-based indices: **0,1,2,3**...

Each row can have multiple child rows. Child row can be collapsed or expanded.

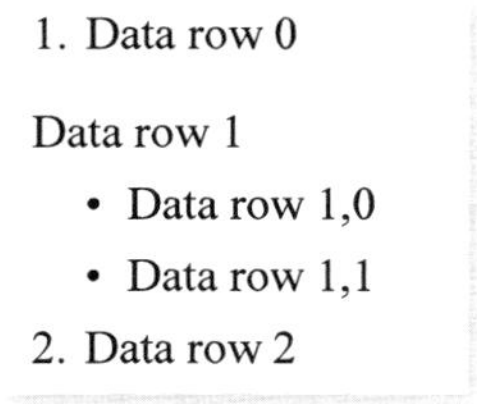
1. Data row 0
Data row 1
• Data row 1,0
• Data row 1,1
2. Data row 2

Attribute	Value	Description
disabled	{boolean}	Disabled *datagrid*.
multiple	{boolean}	Selected multiple rows.

<datalist> [5]

```
Enter phone type:
<input type=text list=fone>

<datalist id=fone>
<option value=Home label=main>
<option value=Office>
<option value=Mobile>
</datalist>
```

The *datalist* element provides an auto complete function on input elements. It enables you to provide a drop down list of predefined options to the user as they input data. This element is not currently supported by major browsers, except for Opera 10.

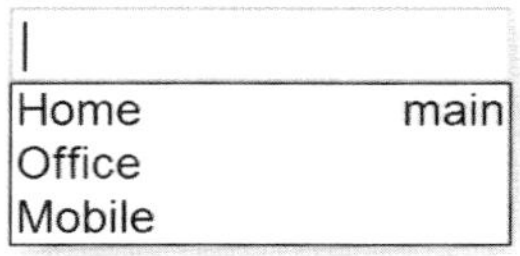
Home
main
Office
Mobile

Attribute	Value	Description
data [5]	{URL}	Automatically populates *datalist* via URL to a well-formed XML file.

<dd>

```
<dl>
<dt>CRT
<dd>Cathode Ray Tube
<dt>LCD
<dd>Liquid Crystal Display
</dl>
```

Definition description

In HTML5 the closing tag **</dd>** is not required.

Tag	Code Example		Description
<del>	He shall be <del datetime=2009-10-10T19:15-08:00>punished</del> <ins>forgiven</ins>		This element indicates a deleted text. He shall be ~~punished~~ forgiven
	Attribute	Value	Description
	cite	{URL}	Source of the reason for the change
	datetime	{date and time}	Date and Time of the change
<details> [5]	<details open> <p>These details could be expanded and collapsed.</p> </details>		A detail which could be expanded and collapsed.
	Attribute	Value	Description
	open	{boolean}	Indicates opened detail
<dfn>	<dfn>Definition term</dfn>		Definition term
	Attribute	Value	Description
	title	{text string}	The text string value must be equal to the definition.
<dir>			Deprecated in HTML5
<div>	<div style=padding:15px> <p>Hello, world!</p> </div>		*div* is a division or section in a document. *div* is utilized to apply styles, classes and JavaScript events to a group of elements. *div* is a generic container which does not carry any semantic information. *div* is a block-level section unlike the *span* element, which is an inline section.
<dl>	<dl> <dt>CRT <dd>Cathode Ray Tube <dt>LCD <dd>Liquid Crystal Display </dl>		Definition list
<dt>			Definition term
<em>	The <em>emphasized</em> text		Emphasized (italicized) text

Tag	Code Example		Description
<embed> [5]	`<embed src=AdBanner.swf>`		Embedded media, content or plug-in
	Attribute	**Value**	**Description**
	height	{pixels}	Height of the content
	src	{URL}	URL of the content
	type	{type}	Type of the content
	width	{pixels}	Width of the content

<fieldset>	`label{width:120px; float:left; text-align:right; display:block; margin-right:0.5em;}`
	
	`<fieldset name=fSet disabled>`
	`<legend>Address</legend>`
	`<p><label>Street</label><input>`
	`<p><label>City</label><input>`
	`<p><label>Zip Code</label><input>`
	`</fieldset>`
			A group of related form elements 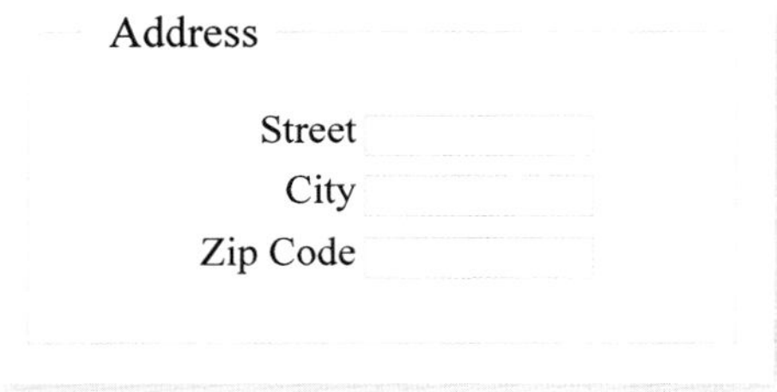

	Attribute	**Value**	**Description**
	disabled [5]	{boolean}	Fieldset visibility
	form [5]	{text string}	Forms associated with fieldset
	name [5]	{text string}	Fieldset name

<figcaption> [5]	`<figure>`
	` <figcaption>CRT</figcaption>`
	` <p>Cathode Ray Tube</p>`
	`</figure>`
			Caption for the *figure* element

<figure> [5]			Figure tag annotates videos, illustrations, photos, etc.
<font>			Deprecated in HTML5

<footer> [5]	`<html><head></head>`
	`<body>`
	`  <section>Content</section>`
	`  <footer>`
	`    2010 © Mavrody`
	`  </footer>`
	`</body>`
	`</html>`
			Section / page footer is a layout element

Tag	Code Example	Description

`<form>`	`<form action=action.asp accept-charset=UTF-8 accept-charset=windows-1252>`
	
	`Card Number <input type=text name=number value=123456789>`
	
	`Expiration <input type=text name=date value=01/01/01>`
	
	`<input type=submit value=Submit></form>`
		Form definition
		
		The following form-associated elements could be nested inside the `<form>` tags:
		
		`<input>`, `<textarea>`, `<button>`, `<select>`, `<option>`, `<optgroup>`, `<fieldset>`, `<datalist>`, `<output>`, `<label>`

	Attribute	Value	Description
	accept	{MIME type}	Not supported in HTML 5
	accept-charset	unknown (default), {text string}	A comma delimited list of possible character sets
	action	{URL}	URL where the data is sent
	autocomplete	{boolean}	Form auto-fill
	enctype	application/x-www-form-urlencoded (default), multipart/form-data, text/plain	Indicates how form data should be encoded prior to sending By default data is encoded so that spaces are converted to (+) symbols, and special characters are converted to the ASCII HEX equivalents.
	method	get (default), post, put, delete	*get* - sends the form data via the URL: {URL} ? name = value & name = value *post* - sends the form data in the body of the request
	name	{text string}	Unique form name
	novalidate ❺	{boolean}	Defines when the form is not validated
	target	_blank, _parent, _self, _top	Where to open the target URL ■ *_blank*: new window ■ *_self*: same frame ■ *_parent*: parent frameset ■ *_top*: full body of the window

Tag	Code Example	Description
`<frame>`, `<frameset>`		Deprecated in HTML5
`<h1>` to `<h6>`	`<h1>Article heading</h1>` `<h2>Article subheading</h2>`	Heading 1 (largest) to Heading 6 (smallest)

Tag	Code Example	Description
<head>	<html> <head> <title>Page Title</title> </head> <body> Page content. </body> </html>	Head of HTML document Head can include the following tags: **<base>**, **<link>**, **<meta>**, **<script>**, **<style>**, **<title>**.
<header> [5]	<header> <h1>iPhone vs. Android</h1> <p>Another Comparo</p> </header> <article></article>	Section / page header
<hgroup> [5]	<header> <hgroup> <h1>iPhone vs. Android</h1> <h2>Another Comparo</h2> </hgroup>	Document of section header definition, used to group a set of **<h1>-<h6>** elements when the heading has multiple levels.
<hr>	<hr>	Horizontal rule
<html>	<!DOCTYPE HTML> <html> <head> <title>Page Title</title> </head> <body>Page content</body> </html>	HTML document definition All HTML elements are nested inside of html container, except for the **<!DOCTYPE HTML>** element which is located before the opening HTML tag.

Attribute	Value	Description
manifest [5]	{URL}	Document's cache URL
xmlns	http://www.w3.org/1999/xhtml	XML namespace attribute. required for XHTM serialization.

Tag	Code Example	Description
<i>	British appartment is known as <i>flat</i>.	An alternate content usually rendered in italics. To markup text with stress emphasis use the *em* element.

Tag	Code Example		Description
`<iframe>`	`<iframe src=http://www.` `aeather.com/chicago></iframe>`		In-line frame that embeds another HTML document

	Attribute	Value	Description
	frameborder	1, 0	Deprecated in HTML5
	height	{number} pixels, %	*iframe* height
	ongdesc	{URL}	Deprecated in HTML 5
	marginheight	{number} pixels	Deprecated in HTML 5
	marginwidth	{number} pixels	Deprecated in HTML 5
	name	{text string}	Unique *iframe* name
	sandbox ❺	allow-forms allow-same-origin allow-scripts	*iframe* content restrictions
	scrolling	yes, no, auto	Deprecated in HTML 5
	seamless ❺	{boolean}	*iframe* borders and scroll bars will not render
	src	{URL}	The URL of the document to show in the *iframe*
	srcdoc ❺	{HTML code}	The HTML of the document showing in the *iframe*
	width	{number} px, %	*iframe* width

Tag	Code Example		Description
`<img>`	`<img src=map.gif alt="Map of` `the North America" width=200>`		External image

	Attribute	Value	Description
	alt	{text string}	Short description of the image, text alternative for assistive technologies
	src	{URL}	Reference to the image location
	height	{number} pixels, %	Height of an image
	ismap	{URL}	Server-side image map
	usemap	{URL}	URL of an image map
	width	{number} pixels, %	Sets the width of an image

Tag	Code Example		Description
`<input>`	`<input name=ssn required autocomplete=on>`		User-editable data control
	Attribute	**Value**	**Description**
	accept	audio/*	A comma-delimited list of MIME types
		video/*	Valid only with `type=file`
		image/*	
		{a MIME type with no parameters}	
	alt	{text string}	Short description of the image. Valid only with `type=image`
	action	{file URL}	URL of the file to process the input
	autocomplete	on (default) off	If "on", browser will store form's input values and auto-fill the form if the page.
	autofocus ❺	{boolean}	Focus on the input field
			Invalid with `type=hidden`
	checked	{boolean}	Indicates that the input element should be checked when it first loads.
			Valid with `type=checkbox` and `type=radio`
	disabled	{boolean}	Disables the input element so that the user can not write text in it, or select it.
			Cannot be used with `type=hidden`.
	form ❺	{text string}	Associates control with one or more form IDs
	formaction ❺	{URL}	Overrides the form's action attribute
	formenctype ❺	application/x-www-form-urlencoded	Overrides the form's *enctype* attribute
		multipart/form-data	
		text/plain	

Tag	Code Example		Description
	formmethod [5]	get post put delete	Overrides the form's method attribute
	formnovalidate [5]	true false	Overrides the form's *novalidate* attribute
	formtarget [5]	_blank _self _parent _top	Overrides the form's target attribute, where to open the target URL. ■ *_blank*: new window ■ *_self*: same frame ■ *_parent*: parent frameset ■ *_top*: full body of the window
	height [5]	{number} pixels, %	Height of an input field
	list [5]	{datalist_id}	Reference to a drop down data list with predefined options.
	max [5]	{number}	Field's maximum legal value
	maxlength	{number}	Input field's maximum number of characters allowed
	min [5]	{number}	Field's minimum legal value
	multiple [5]	{boolean}	Multiple values allowed
	name	{text string}	Field's unique name
	pattern [5]	{text string: JavaScript pattern}	Specifies a regular expression against which the control's value is to be checked.
	placeholder [5]	{text string}	Short hint such as a sample value or a brief description of the expected format.
	readonly	{boolean}	Value of the field is not editable

Tag	Code Example		Description
	required ❺	{boolean}	Required input field. This attribute cannot be used with the types: hidden, image, button, submit, reset.

			```[required] {```
			```border-color: #88a;```
			
			```-webkit-box-shadow: 0 0 3px rgba(0, 0, 255, .5);}```
			
			```<input required>```

	size	{number}	Length of the field measured by number of visible characters
	src	{URL}	URL of the image when input `type=image`
	step ❺	{number} any	Specifies the required granularity of the value, by limiting the allowed values. This attribute is legal when `type=date`, `datetime`, `datetime-local`, `month`, `week`, `time`, `number`, or `range`.
	type ❺	button, checkbox, color, date, datetime, datetime-local, email, file, hidden, image, month, number, password, radio, range, reset, search, submit, tel, text, time, url, week	Element type. HTML5 *input* element introduced several new values for the *type* attribute, described in the previous Web Forms 2.0 section of this chapter.
	value	{text string}	■ Initial control value ■ Illegal with `type=file` ■ Required for *checkbox* and *radio* button input
	width ❺	{number} pixels, %	Width of the input field
`<ins>`	`<ins>`Date`</ins>` of the insertion		Inserted text
	Attribute	Value	Description
	cite	{URL}	A URL to an additional info
	datetime	{yyyy/mm/dd}	Date and time of the insertion
`<kbd>`	Type `<kbd>`www.ebay.com`</kbd>` into browser address bar.		Keyboard text entered by user

Tag	Code Example	Description

<keygen> [5]

```
<form action=processkey.cgi
method=post enctype=multipart/
form-data>
 <p><keygen name=mykey>
 <p><input type=submit
value="Submit this key">

</form>
```

The *keygen* element represents a control for generating a public-private key pair and for submitting the public key from that pair.

Attribute	Value	Description
autofocus	{boolean}	Sets focus on the button when the page loads.
challenge	{boolean}	If present, the value of the *keygen* is set to be challenged when submitted.
disabled	{boolean}	Disables the input element when it first loads so that the user cannot write text in it, or select it.
form	{text string}	Unique form name the input field belongs to.
keytype	{rsa}	Key type definition. RSA is a signature algorithm for public key encryption.
name	{text string}	Unique element name.

<label>

```
label {
width:120px; float:left;
text-align:right; display:block;
margin-right:0.5em;}

<p><label for=str>Street</label>
<input id=str>

<p><label for=city>City</label>
<input id=city>

<p><label for=zip>Zip Code</label>
<input id=zip>
```

The *label* element uses unique id to associate label with input for usability and accessibility applications. You can also assign CSS properties to it.

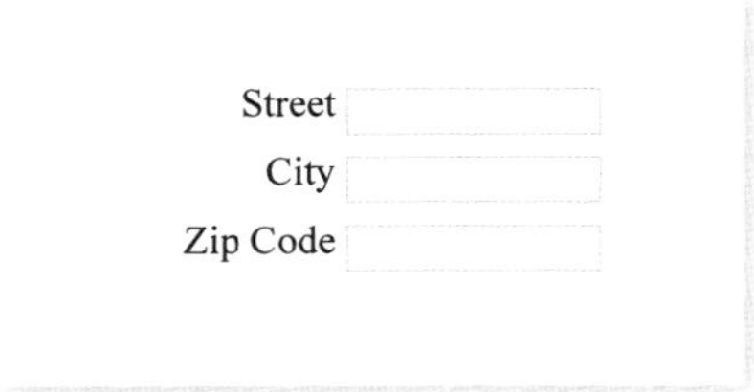

Attribute	Value	Description
for	{id}	Defines label/input association. If this attribute is not present, the label is associated with its contents.
form	{text string}	Unique form name. Defines label/ forms association.

Tag	Code Example	Description

`<legend>`	`<fieldset>`
	`<legend>Address</legend>`
	`  <p>Street <input type=text>`
	`  <p>City <input type=text>`
	`  <p>Zip Code <input`
	`type=text>`
	`</fieldset>`
		The *legend* element provides title for the *fieldset*, *figure*, and the *details* elements.
		
		<div align=center>Address</div>
		<div align=center>Street</div>

Tag	Code Example	Description

`<li>`	`<ol>`
	`  <li>New York`
	`  <li>Los Angeles`
	`  <li>Chicago`
	`</ol>`
		List item. Closing tag `</li>` is not required in HTML5.

Attribute	Value	Description
value	{number}	Value of the first list item within the *ol* element.

Tag	Code Example	Description

`<link>` ❺	`<head>`
	`    <link rel=stylesheet`
	`type=text/css href=style.css>`
	`</head>`
		Link to external resource. It must appear in the head of the document and it is usually used to point to a style sheets file.

Attribute	Value	Description
href	{URL}	The URL of the resource
hreflang	{language code}	Language definition
media	screen, tty, tv, projection, handheld, print, braille, aural, all	Type of device the document designed for. ■ *screen* - Computer screens ■ *tty* - Teletypes and terminals ■ *tv* - Televisions ■ *projection* - Projectors ■ *handheld* - Handhelds ■ *print* - For document on-screen viewing, print preview, and printed output ■ *braille* - Braille devices ■ *aural* - Speech synthesizers ■ *all* - All devices

Tag	Code Example		Description
	rel	alternate, archives, author, first, help, icon, index, last, license, next, pingback, prefetch, prev, search, stylesheet, sidebar, tag, up	■ Relationship between the document and the destination URL ■ The *href* attribute must be present ■ Accepts multiple values, separated by a space
	sizes	{number}	Sizes of the linked resource when `rel=icon`.
	type	{mime type}	Specifies the Multipurpose Internet Mail Extensions type of the target URL. This attribute requires the *href* attribute

| `<map>` | `<img src =shapes.gif width=166 height=132 alt=shapes usemap=#shapemap>`

`<map name=shapemap>`
`<area shape=rect coords=0,0,60,90 href=square. htm alt=square>`
`</map>` | | ■ Client-side image-map with clickable areas.
■ The *name* attribute is required in the map element. |

	Attribute	Value	Description
	name	{text string}	Unique name

| `<mark>` ❺ | `<p>The <mark>name</mark> attribute is required.</p>` | | Marked text or highlighted text

The **name** attribute is required. |

| `<menu>` | `<menu label=stars>`
`  <li><input type=radio>Sun`
`  <li><input type=radio>Alpha`
`</menu>` | | Menu list. Typically it contains form controls |

	Attribute	Value	Description
	label	{text string}	Defines a visible label for the menu
	type	context,toolbar, list	Menu type

Tag	Code Example	Description

`<meta>`	```<!DOCTYPE HTML>```
	```<html><head>```
	```<title>Title</title>```
	
	```<meta name=keywords```
	```content="HTML5, CSS3, RDF">```
	
	```</head><body></body></html>```
		Meta information about page: refresh rates, character encoding, author, descriptions, keywords for search engines.

Attribute	Value	Description
charset	{character encoding}	Character encoding declaration
content	{text string}	Meta information associated with *http-equiv* or *name*
http-equiv	{content-language}, {content-type}, {default-style}, {expires}, {refresh}, {set-cookie}	HTTP message header attribute
name	author, description, keywords, generator, revised, others	Property name

Tag	Code Example	Description
`<meter>` ❺	```<meter min=0 max=100 value=50>``` ```</meter>```	Predefined measurement range, but not a single number

Shipment Status

Attribute	Value	Description
high	{number}	High range limit
low	{number}	Low range limit
max	{number}	Maximum value. Default is **1**
min	{number}	Minimum value. Default is **0**
optimum	{number}	■ Measurement's value is the best value. Higher then the "high" value indicates that the higher value is better ■ Lower than the "low" value indicates that the lower value is better ■ The in between value indicates that neither high nor low values are good
value	{number}	Measured value

Tag	Code Example	Description
<nav> [5]	<nav> <a href=index.html>Home</a> <a href=products.htm> Products</a> <a href=contact.htm> Contacts</a> </nav>	Layout element which defines navigational section
<noframes>		Deprecated in HTML5
<noscript>	<script src=script.js type="text/javascript"> </script> <noscript>This browser does not support JavaScript</noscript>	*noscript* section. It defines alternate content for browsers that recognizes the *script* element, but does not support the script in it.
<object>	<object type=video/quicktime data=wedding.mov width=380 height=320></object>	Embedded object such as image, audio, video, Java applet, ActiveX, Flash or PDF.

Attribute	Value	Description
data	{URL}	URL to the object's data
form	{text string}	Form this button related to
height, width	{number} pixels	Height, width of the object
name	{text string}	Unique object name
type	{MIME_type}	Multipurpose Internet Mail Extensions type of the target URL. This attribute requires the *href* attribute
usemap	{URL}	URL of the image map
align	left, right, top, bottom	Deprecated in HTML5
archive	{URL}	
border	{number} pixels	
classid	{text_string}	
codebase	{URL}	
codetype	{MIME_type}	
declare	{boolean}	
hspace	{number} pixels	
standby	text	
vspace	{number} pixels	

Tag	Code Example	Description

`<ol>`	```<ol start=3>```
	  ```<li>Mars```
	  ```<li>Jupiter```
	  ```<li>Saturn```
	```</ol>```
		Ordered list
		
		3. Mars
		4. Jupiter
		5. Saturn

Attribute	Value	Description
reversed ❺	{boolean}	Descending list order
start	{number}	Initial list number

Tag	Code Example	Description

`<optgroup>`	```<select>```
	```<optgroup label=fruits>```
	  ```<option>Apple```
	  ```<option>Peach```
	```<optgroup label=veggies>```
	  ```<option>Tomato```
	  ```<option>Onion```
	```</select>```
		Group of related options in a select list. Closing tag `</optgroup>` is not required in HTML5.
		
		Peach
		fruits
		  Apple
		  Peach
		veggies
		  Tomato
		  Onion

Attribute	Value	Description
label	{text string}	Option group label
disabled	{boolean}	Disables option group options

Tag	Code Example	Description

`<option>`	```<select>```
	  ```<option>Apple```
	  ```<option>Peach```
	```</select>```
		Drop-down list option
		
		Closing tag `</option>` is not required in HTML5.

Attribute	Value	Description
disabled	{boolean}	Disabled option
label	{text string}	Alternative label to the option item
selected	{boolean}	Initially selected option
value	{text string}	Initial value of the option item

Tag	Code Example	Description
`<output>` ❺	```<form action=myAction.asp>``` ```<output name=total></output>```	Output element definition. Could be used for data calculations

Attribute	Value	Description
for	id of another element	Element association
form	{text string}	Forms association
name	{text string}	Unique object name for the form

Tag	Code Example	Description
`<p>`	`<p>`Paragraph text`</p>`	Paragraph

`<param>`	`<object type=application.edo>`
	  `<param name=ac_1 value=abc>`
	`This page requires the use`
	`of plug-in</object>`
		Object parameter

Attribute	Value	Description
name	{text string}	Defines a unique name for the parameter. Required attribute.
value	{text string}	Specifies the value of the parameter. Required attribute.

Tag	Code Example	Description

`<pre>`	`<pre>`This text should be
	    displayed preserving
	spacing and ignoring
	word
	    wrap
	`</pre>`
		Pre-formatted text. Text is displayed in a fixed-width font such as Courier, preserving spacing and ignoring word wrap.

`<progress>` ⑤	Downloading now. please wait...
	
	`<progress value=30 max=100>`
	  `<span id=downl>`30`</span>`%
	`</progress>`
		Animated task in-progress indication
		
		Downloading now. please wait...

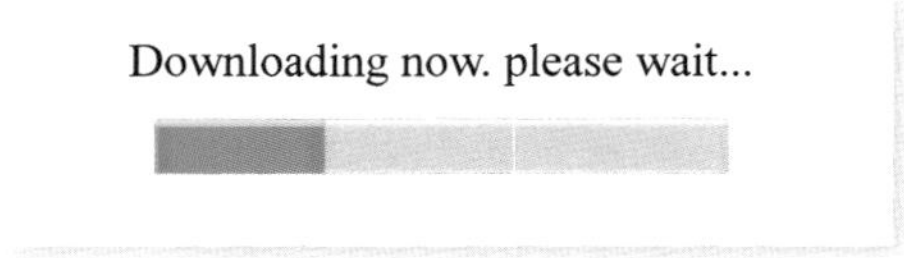

Attribute	Value	Description
max	{number}	Task completion measurement
value	{number}	Overall task measurement

Tag	Code Example	Description
`<q>`	`<p>`The phrase `<q cite=http://` `en.wikipedia.org>`to be, or not to be`</q>` comes from William Shakespeare's Hamlet.`</p>`	Quotation The phrase to "be, or not to be" comes from William Shakespeare's Hamlet.

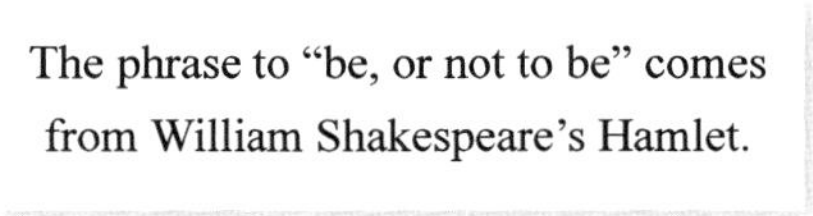

Attribute	Value	Description
cite	{URL}	Quotation source

Tag	Code Example	Description
`<rp>` 5	```<ruby>``` 蘋果 ```<rt>``` ```<rp>(</rp>apple<rp>)</rp>``` ```</rt>``` ```</ruby>```	Ruby annotations to define what to show browsers that to not support the ruby element. Example: **apple** 蘋果
`<rt>` 5		Chinese ruby pronunciation annotation
`<ruby>` 5		Ruby annotations definition
`<s>`		Deprecated in HTML5
`<samp>`	`<samp>return{find(chars.begin())!=chars.end()}</samp>`	Sample programming code. Most browsers display the `<samp>` tag in a so called 'monospace' font - usually Courier New.
`<script>`	```<script type=text/javascript defer src=common.js>``` ``` function goMain() { window.location="main.jsp";}``` ```</script>```	Client-side script definition

Attribute	Value	Description
async 5	{boolean}	Asynchronous script execution
type	text/ecmascript text/javascript application/ecmascript application/javascript text/vbscript	Script MIME type
charset	charset	Script character encoding
defer	{boolean}	Script execution time options: - Immediately (default) - After the page has rendered
src	{URL}	Target URL to an external JavaScript file

Tag	Code Example	Description

<section> [5]

```
<article>
  <header>
     <h1>ABC Interactive</h1>
  </header>

  <section>
     <h2>Services</h2><p></p>
  </section>

  <section>
     <h2>Location</h2><p></p>
  </section>
</article>
```

Layout section definition

<select>

```
<select>

  <option>Visa
  <option>Master Card
  <option>American Express

</select>
```

Selectable drop down list

Attribute	Value	Description
autofocus [5]	{boolean}	Places focus on the input field
disabled	{boolean}	Disables the list
form [5]	{text string}	Form association
multiple	{boolean}	Multiple items can be selected
name	{text string}	Unique list name
size	{number}	Visible number of the list items

<small>

```
<footer>
<small>2010 © Mavrody</small>
</footer>
```

Small element usually utilized for a fine print and legal disclaimers.

<source> [5]

```
<video controls autoplay>

 <source src=mymovie.mp4
 type='video/mp4;
 codecs="theora, vorbis"'>

 <source src=mymovie.ogv
 type='video/ogg;
 codecs="avc1.42E, mp4a.40"'>

</video>
```

Multiple media source for *video* and *audio* elements. If the media attribute is omitted, it is the default: the media resource is for all media.

The *codecs* parameter may need to be assigned to specify the resource encoding.

Attribute	Value	Description
media	media query	Type of media resource, for browsers to decide if it shall download it or not

Tag	Code Example		Description
	src	{URL}	The URL of the media
	type	{mime type}	Multipurpose Internet Mail Extensions type of the embedded content

`<span>`	```<div>```
	
	```The <span style=color:blue> span tag</span> is utilized to apply styles, classes and <span class=index>JavaScript </span> events to a text string or to a group of elements.```
	
	```</div>```
			span is a section in a document. span is utilized to apply styles, classes and JavaScript events to a text string or to a group of elements.
			
			■ 'span' is a generic container which does not carry any semantic information.
			
			■ 'span' is an *inline*-level section unlike the 'div' element, which is a *block*-level section.

`<strike>`			Deprecated in HTML5
`<strong>`	```This is a matter of a great <strong>importance</strong>, while <strong>this matter even <strong>more important </strong></strong>```		Strong importance indicator. This element could be nested to emphasize stronger importance.

`<style>`	```<!DOCTYPE html>```
	```<html><head><title></title>```
	
	``` <style type=text/css>```
	``` p {color:blue;}```
	``` </style>```
	
	```</head>```
	```<body>```
	
	``` <p>Blue paragraph</p>```
	
	``` <div>```
	
	``` <style type=text/css```
	``` media=screen scoped>```
	``` p {color:green;}```
	``` </style>```
	
	``` <p>Green paragraph</p>```
	
	``` </div>```
			Defines page-level *Cascading Style Sheets* classes, as opposed to an external CSS file.
			
			■ Style element usually appear inside the *head* element
			
			■ The *scoped* attribute is required if the *style* element placed within the *body* element

Attribute	Value	Description
type	text/css	Content-type

Tag	Code Example		Description
	media	screen tty tv projection handheld print braille aural all	Type of device the document designed for ■ *screen* - Computer screens ■ *tty* - Teletypes and terminals ■ *tv* - Televisions ■ *projection* - Projectors ■ *handheld* - Handhelds ■ *print* - For document on-screen viewing, print preview, and printed output ■ *braille* - Braille devices ■ *aural* - Speech synthesizers ■ *all* - All devices
	scoped [5]	{boolean}	The HTML5 *scoped* attribute applies styles to a parent element. If this attribute is not present, styles will be applied to the whole document. At the time of writing no browsers have implemented the attribute yet.
<sub>	Water is a substance with chemical formula H**_{**2**}**O		Defines subscripted text which could be used in mathematical expressions and in some languages. Water is a substance with chemical formula H_2O
<summary> [5]	<details> **<summary>**Design**</summary>** This article is about the general concept of design. </details>		'Summary' is a header for the *detail* element
<sup>	The amount of energy is directly proportional to the mass of body: E = mc**^{**2**}**		*sub* defines superscripted text which could be used for mathematical expressions, symbols, and in some languages. The amount of energy is directly proportional to the mass of body: $E = mc^2$

Tag	Code Example	Description
`<table>`	```<table summary=contribution>``` ```<tr>``` ```<th>1st column header cell``` ```<th>2nd column header cell``` ```<tr>``` ```<td>1st row, 1st cell``` ```<td>1st row, 2nd cell``` ```</table>```	*Table* element typically represents 2-dimentional data, in the form of grid of cells. ■ Tables should not be used to control page layout ■ Initially there has been a debate about possible removal of the *summary* attribute

Attribute	Value	Description
summary	{text string}	Table content summary
border	{number} pixels	Deprecated in HTML5
cellpadding		
cellspacing		
frame	void, above, below, hsides, lhs, rhs, vsides, box, border	
rules	none, groups, rows, cols, all	
width	{number} pixels, %	

Tag	Code Example	Description
`<thead>`	```<table summary=payments>``` ```<thead class=hd>``` ```<tr>``` ```<th>Name``` ```<th>Amount``` ```</thead>```	*t-header*, *t-body* and *t-footer* elements utilized to group table cells for a CSS control over a group. ■ If you use one of these 3 elements, you should use all of them ■ The following apply to each of the 3 elements: - Must have a `<tr>` tag inside - Closing tags are optional - Global attributes supported - Element-specific attributes are deprecated: align, char, charoff, valign ■ The `<td>` tag is illegal inside of the *t-header* element
`<tbody>`	```<tbody class=bd>``` ```<tr>``` ```<td>John``` ```<td>$100``` ```<tr>``` ```<td>Ann``` ```<td>$50``` ```</tbody>```	
`<tfoot>`	```<tfoot class=ft>``` ```<tr>``` ```<td>Total``` ```<td>$150``` ```</tfoot>``` ```</table>```	

Name	Amount
John	$100
Ann	$50
Total	**$150**

Tag	Code Example	Description

`<td>`	`<table>`
	
	`<tr>`
	`<th` *colspan*`=3 id=`**cont**`>Contact`
	
	`<tr>`
	`<th id=`**fn**`>First Name`
	`<th id=`**ln**`>Last Name`
	`<th id=`**ph**`>Phone`
	
	`<tr>`
	`<td` *headers*`='cont fn'>John`
	`<td` *headers*`='cont ln'>Smith`
	`<td` *headers*`='cont ph'>312235`
	
	`</table>`
		Table cell
		
		■ Closing `</td>` tag is not required
		■ The code example illustrates use of attributes *colspan* and *headers*.

Contact		
First Name	**Last Name**	**Phone**
John	Smith	312-235-5678
Ann	Jackson	202-123-4567

Attribute	Value	Description
headers	{text string}	Accessibility attribute - text string consisting of an unordered set of unique space-separated header IDs
colspan	{number}	Number of columns this cell spans
rowspan	{number}	Number of rows this cell spans
abbr	{text string}	Deprecated in HTML5
align	left, right, center, justify, char	
axis	{text string}	
char	character	
charoff	{number}	
height	{number} pixels, %	
nowrap	{boolean}	
nowrap	{boolean}	
scope	col, colgroup, row, rowgroup	
valign	top, middle, bottom...	

Tag	Code Example		Description
`<textarea>`	`<textarea rows=5 cols=10>` `To be or not to be</textarea>`		Multi-line text area

	Attribute	Value	Description
	autofocus **5**	{boolean}	Places focus on the input field. Invalid with `type="hidden"`.
	cols	{number}	Number of characters visible in a sigle row of the text-area
	disabled	{boolean}	Disables the input element when it first loads so that the user can not write text in it, or select it. Cannot be used with `type=hidden`
	form **5**	{text string}	Associates control with form ID(s)
	maxlength **5**	{number}	Maximum number of characters allowed
	name	{text string}	Field's unique name
	placeholder **5**	{text string}	Short hint such as a sample value or a brief description of the expected format.
	readonly	{boolean}	Value of the field is not editable
	required **5**	{boolean}	Defines a required input field's. This attribute cannot be used with the following types: hidden, image, button, submit, reset
	rows	{number}	Number of rows in the text-area
	wrap **5**	hard, soft	Content wrapping type ▪ The *hard* type takes advantage of the *cols* attribute to set line breaks ▪ The *soft* type adds no line breaks

Tag	Code Example		Description
`<th>`	`<tr><th>Header</th></tr>`		Table header cell

	Attribute	Value	Description
	colspan, rowspan	{number}	Indicates the number of columns/rows this cell should span
	scope	col, colgroup, row, rowgroup	Header cells that will use this header's information

Tag	Code Example		Description
	abbr	{text string}	Deprecated in HTML5
	align	left, right, center...	
	axis	{text string}	
	char	character	
	charoff	{number}	
	height	{number} pixels, %	
	nowrap	{boolean}	
	valign	top, middle, bottom...	
	width	{number} pixels, %	
<time> [5]	The Apollo 11 landed the first humans on the Moon on <time datetime="1969-07-20T17:40"> July 20, 1969 at 20:17:40</time>		Date/time element
	Attribute	**Value**	**Description**
	datetime	{datetime}	Specifies the date or time that the element represents in any one of the following formats: ■ Date: **1995-12-30** ■ Time: **23:59** **23:59:12** **23:59:12.30** ■ Date and time: - 'Z' is a time zone designator - Date and time separated by 'T' **1995-12-30T23:59** **1995-12-30T23:59:58Z** **1995-12-30T23:59:58-08:00**
<title>	<head> <title>Google</title> </head>		HTML document title, appears in the browser's tab/title bar 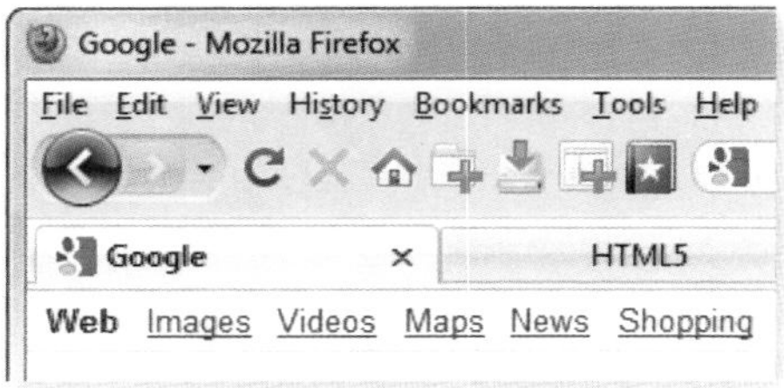

Tag	Code Example	Description

`<tr>`	`<table>`
	 `<tr>`
	 `<td>Cell1</td><td>Cell2</td>`
	 `</tr>`
	`</table>`
		Table row
		
		Attributes deprecated in HTML5:
		align, char, charoff, valign

`<tt>`		Deprecated in HTML5
`<u>`		

`<ul>`	`<ul>`
	  `<li>Mars`
	  `<li>Jupiter`
	  `<li>Saturn`
	`</ul>`
		Unordered (or un-numbered) list which is typically rendered as a series of bulleted items.

`<var>`	`I expect at least <var>n</var> number of guests to arrive.`	Variable
`<video>` ❺	`<video src=mymovie.vid controls autoplay loop preload>`This video is not supported by your browser`</video>`	Video

Attribute	Value	Description
autoplay	{boolean}	Video plays automatically
controls	{boolean}	Video controls displayed
height	{number} pixels	Height of the video player
loop	{boolean}	Video plays unlimited loop
preload	{boolean}	Video loaded at page load and ready to play
src	{URL}	URL of the video
width	{number} pixels	Width of the video player

Tag	Code Example	Description
`<xmp>`		Deprecated in HTML5

HTML5 Forms aka Web Forms 2.0

Web Forms 2.0 draft specification was superseded by HTML5 Forms specification. Form elements and attributes in HTML5 provide a higher degree of semantics vs. HTML4 while also offering a simplified markup and user interface styling.

A wide range of web forms functionality is now available without the use of JavaScript, Ajax libraries or plugin-based technologies, utilizing the updated HTML markup.

This section provides an overview of new input element types and attributes and the next chapter offers a more complete summary.

HTML5 <input> **types and attributes**

<table>
<tr><th>Type</th><th>Description</th><th>Example</th></tr>
<tr><td>date [5]</td><td>ISO 8601 encoded year, month, and day.
Format: yyyy-mm-dd

The screenshot example is rendered by Opera for Windows.

<code><input type=date></code></td><td>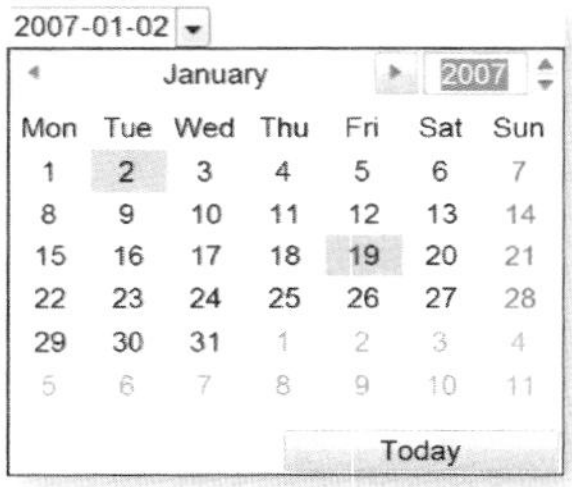
</td></tr>
<tr><td>datetime [5]

datetime-local [5]</td><td>Datetime type allows for user selection of a date and time: ISO 8601 encoded year, month, day, hour, minute, second, fractions of a second, and expressed in UTC, the Coordinated Universal Time.
Format: yyyy-mm-dd HH:MMZ

The datetime-local type displays no timezone. Format: yyyy-mm-dd HH:MM

<code><input type=datetime></code></td><td>
</td></tr>
<tr><td>month [5]</td><td>ISO 8601 encoded year, and a month.
Format: yyyy-mm

<code><input type=month></code></td><td>
</td></tr>
</table>

Type	Description	Example
week ⑤	ISO 8601 encoded year, and a week. Format: yyyy-mmW `<input type=week>`	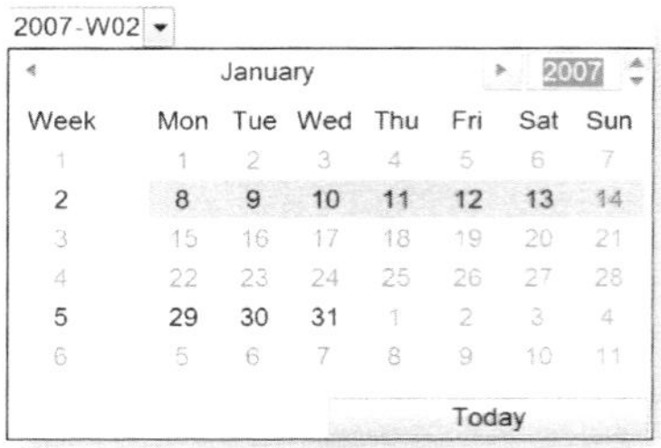
color ⑤	Color picker control. ■ **placeholder** ⑤ attribute represents a hint text intended to aid the user with data entry `<input type=color placeholder=black>`	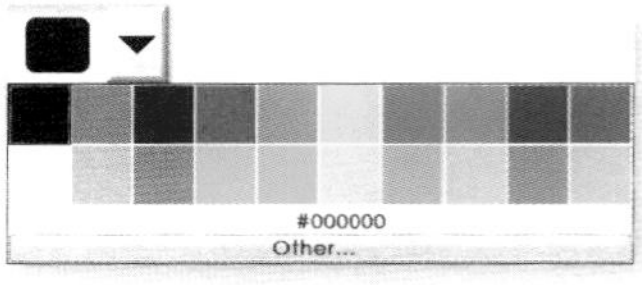
tel ⑤	Telephone number. ■ **placeholder** ⑤ attribute represents a hint text intended to aid the user with data entry ■ **pattern** ⑤ attribute defines a regular expression against which the control's value is to be validated	 `<input type=tel` *placeholder*=" (000)000-0000" *pattern*="^\(?\d{3}\)?[-\s]\d{3}[-\s]\d{4}.*?$">` (000)000-0000
time ⑤	Hour, minute, seconds, fractional seconds. `<input type=time>`	10:21
range ⑤	'Range' slider widget contains a value from a range of numbers. ■ **min** and **max** ⑤ attributes indicate the defined range of values for the element	`<input type=range` *min*=5 *max*=10>`
search ⑤	'Search' input. ■ **placeholder** ⑤ attribute as a hint ■ **autofocus** ⑤ attribute gives field instant focus ■ **results** attribute gives a drop down with the number of results requested. It is not an HTML5 attribute: it is *Webkit* browser specific only.	`<input type=search results=5` *autofocus placeholder*=Search...>` Search... html5 ✕

Type	Description	Example
number [5]	Accepts numerical value only. ■ **step** [5] attribute specifies the increment input can be updated ■ **min** and **max** [5] attributes indicate the defined range of values ■ **value** attribute sets the initial value	<input type=number value=20 *step*=1 *min*=5 *max*=50> Hours: 20
email [5]	Accepts email value only. ■ **required** [5] attribute could simplify input validation code and error styling ■ **oninvalid** [5] event can be used for validations	input[required] { background: yellow;} input:invalid { background-color:orange; border: 2px red solid;} input:valid { border: 1px solid green;} <input type=email required> Email myemail@domain
url [5]	Accepts URL value only ■ **list** [5] atribute can retrieve predefined values ■ New *datalist* [5] element can store values for the **list** attribute	<input type=url list=link_set name=link> <datalist id=link_set> <option label=Orbitz value=http://www.orbitz.com> <option label=Kayak value=http://www.kayak.com> </datalist> http://www.orbitz.com Orbitz http://www.kayak.com Kayak http://www.expedia.com Expedia

HTML5 <output> **element**

Element	Description	Example
output [5]	**<output>** is HTML5 tag to representing the results of data calculations ■ **onforminput** ia a new form event	<input type=number value=20> <output name=rate onforminput="...">0</output> <output name=total onforminput="...">0</output> 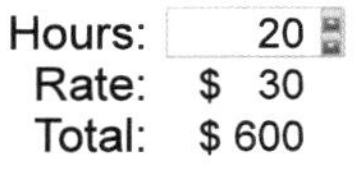Hours: 20 Rate: $ 30 Total: $ 600

<Input> **element type/attribute matrix**

	Text, Search, URL, Tel	Email	Password	Datetime, Date, Week, Month, Time	Number, Datetime-local	Range	Color	Checkbox, Radio	File	Button	Image
accept									✓		
alt											✓
autocomplete	✓	✓	✓	✓	✓	✓	✓				
checked								✓			
files									✓		
formaction										✓	✓
formenctype										✓	✓
formmethod										✓	✓
formnovalidate										✓	✓
formtarget										✓	✓
height, width											✓
list	✓	✓		✓	✓	✓	✓				
max, min				✓	✓	✓					
maxlength	✓	✓	✓								
multiple		✓							✓		
pattern	✓	✓	✓								
placeholder	✓	✓	✓								
readonly	✓	✓	✓	✓	✓						
required	✓	✓	✓	✓	✓			✓	✓		
size	✓	✓	✓								
src											✓
step				✓	✓	✓					
value	✓	✓	✓	✓	✓	✓	✓	✓	✓	✓	✓

HTML5 Browser Compatibility

Elements

	Desktop					Mobile		
	IE	FireFox	Safari	Chrome	Opera	iOS	Opera	Android
Basic Canvas	9	3	3.2	6	10.5	3.2	10	2.1
Audio	9	3.5	4	6	10.5	4	✕	2.3
Video	9	3.5	4	6	10.5	4	✕	2.3
Rubi	9*	4*	6*	6*	11.1?	✕	✕	✕
Semantic Elements	9	4	5	6	11.1*	4	10*	2.1
Form Elements	9?	4*	4*	7	10.5	4*	10	✕
Progress and Meter	9?	4?	6	8	11	✕	✕	✕
Details & Summary	9?	4?	6?	10?	11.1?	✕	✕	✕
Border Radius	9	3	3.2	6	10.5	3.2	✕	2.1*
Text Overflow	6*	4?	3.2*	6*	10.5*	3.2*	10*	2.1*
Multi-column Layout	9?	3	3.2	6	11.1	3.2	✕	2.1
Flexible Box Layout	9?	4	3.2	6	11.1?	3.2	✕	2.1
Media Queries	9	3.5	4	6	10.5	3.2	10	2.1
Advanced Selectors	9	3.5	3.2	6	10.5	3.2	10	2.1
Box-Shadow	9	3.5	3.2	6	10.5	3.2	✕	2.1
Overall compliance	**60%**	**73%**	**82%**	**88%**	**73%**	**73%**	**33%**	**67%**

* indicates partial support

? indicates unknown support

✕ indicates no support

4. Global Attributes and Events

Global Attributes

Summary

- Global attributes apply to all HTML elements with some minor exceptions.
- The code examples use mainly the HTML5 syntax (not XHTML).

Attribute	Value	Sample Code	Description
accesskey [5]	{character}		Keyboard shortcut
class	{text string}	<header **class=title**> Article Heading </header>	Class name in a style sheet
contenteditable [5]	true false	<section **contenteditable**> <p>Edit me!</p> </section>	Specifies if user can edit the content. An elements with the '**contenteditable**' attribute will display a grey dotted outline on roll over.
contextmenu [5]	{text string}	<input name=char type=text **contextmenu=mymenu**> <menu type=context id=mymemenu> <command label="Pick a name" onclick="document.forms.npc.elements.char.value=getRandomName()"> <command label="Prefill other fields based on name" onclick= "prefillFields(document.forms. npc.elements.char.value)"> </menu>	Context menu definition

Attribute	Value	Sample Code	Description
data-{text_string} [5]	{text string}		Custom-defined attributes. Must include prefix '**`data-`**'.
dir	ltr rtl	`<html dir=rtl>`	Text direction: useful in some languages

draggable [5]	true
	false
	auto
		`<div draggable=true>`
		`<menu></menu>`
		`</div>`
			Defines user-dragable capability status

hidden [5]	{boolean}	`<div hidden>`
		`<p>Hidden text`
		`</div>`
			Defines hidden elements

id	{text string}	`<input id=ssn>`	Element's unique id

item [5]	{empty string}
	{text string}
	{URL}
		`item=""`
		`item=dbase`
		`item="http://abc.com/ microdata/"`
			Used for *microdata*

itemprop [5]	{text string}	`<div itemscope>`
		`<p>Las Name`
		`<span itemprop=lname>`
		`Smith </span>`
		`</p>`
		`</div>`
			Defines *microdata* item property

lang	{lang_code}	`<p lang=en>Text</p>`	Language code for the content of an element.

spellcheck [5]	true
	false
	{empty string}
	{empty}
		`<textarea spellcheck=true>`
		`<textarea spellcheck="false">`
		`<textarea spellcheck>`
			Element has "check as you type" feature enabled

style	{text string}	`<p style=heading>`
		`Article Title`
		`</p>`
			Inline style

tabindex	{number}	`<input tabindex=1>`	Tab order
title	{text string}	`<table title="July Flight Schedule">`	Additional info

Global Events

HTML Event Handler Attributes

Most HTML tags can be interacted with by events. There are many of different ways an event can occur, including:

- User interaction using keyboard key press or mouse click
- Automatic page processing, such as page loading.
- At set time-intervals or after a delay.
- JavaScript can be attached to an event using JavaScript *event handler*, which could trigger an action.
- Event Handlers correspond to HTML tag attributes.
- JavaScript defines the five types of events:
  - form
  - keyboard
  - mouse
  - media
  - window

```
<input type=button value=Confirm
onclick="alert('Are you sure?')">
```

Window

Applicable to the **<body>** tag.

Attribute	When script will run
onafterprint [5]	After printing
onbeforeprint [5]	Before printing
onbeforeonload [5]	Before the page loads
onblur	Window loses focus
onerror [5]	An error happen
onfocus	Window gets focus
onhaschange [5]	Page has change
onload	Page loads
onmessage [5]	Message is displayed
onoffline [5]	Page goes offline

Attribute	When script will run
ononline [5]	Page comes online
onpagehide [5]	Window is hidden
onpageshow [5]	Window is shown
onpopstate [5]	Window's history changes. The event offers a way to change the URL displayed in the browser using JavaScript without reloading the page. It will also create a back-button event.
onredo [5]	Redo command is executed
onresize [5]	Window is resized
onstorage [5]	Page loads
onundo [5]	Undo command is executed
onunload [5]	Viewer leaves the page

Form

Global events triggered by actions inside a HTML form. These global events are the most common in form elements.

Attribute	When script will run
onblur	Element loses focus
onchange	Element changes
oncontextmenu [5]	Context menu is activated
onfocus	Element gets focus
onformchange [5]	Form changes
onforminput [5]	User applies input to the form control
oninput [5]	Element has user input
onreset	Deprecated in HTML5
oninvalid [5]	Element is invalid
onselect	Element is selected
onsubmit	Form is submitted

Keyboard

Global events triggered by a keyboard.

Attribute	When script will run
onkeydown	Key is pressed
onkeypress	Key is pressed and released
onkeyup	Key is released

Mouse

Global events triggered by a mouse, or similar user actions.

Attribute	When script will run
onclick	Mouse click
ondblclick	Mouse double-click
ondrag [5]	Element is dragged
ondragend [5]	Element is at the end of a drag process
ondragenter [5]	Element has been dragged and dropped to a valid target
ondragleave [5]	Element leaves a valid drop target
ondragover [5]	Element is dragged over a target
ondragstart [5]	Start of a drag process
ondrop [5]	Dragged element is being dropped
onmousedown	Button is pressed
onmousemove	Mouse pointer moves
onmouseout	Mouse pointer leaves an element
onmouseover	Mouse pointer hovers over an element
onmouseup	Mouse button is released
onmousewheel [5]	Mouse wheel is being turned
onscroll [5]	Scrollbar is being scrolled

Media

These global events triggered by videos, images and audio.

Attribute	When script will run
onabort	Event termination
oncanplay [5]	Buffered event
oncanplaythrough [5]	Buffering is not required for playback
ondurationchange [5]	Playback duration is changed
onemptied [5]	Media resource element is empty due to an error
onended [5]	End of playback
onerror [5]	Element loading error
onloadeddata [5]	Media data is loaded for the first time
onloadedmetadata [5]	Media duration and dimensions data is loaded
onloadstart [5]	Media data starts to load
onpause [5]	Media data is paused
onplay [5]	Media playback has begun
onplaying [5]	Media is in progress
onprogress [5]	Browser is retrieving the media data
onratechange [5]	Media playback rate has changed
onreadystatechange [5]	Ready-state changes
onseeked [5]	Media element's seeking attribute is false
onseeking [5]	Media element's seeking attribute is true: the seeking has started
onstalled [5]	Error in retrieving media data
onsuspend [5]	Media data retrieval has been interrupted
ontimeupdate [5]	Media playing position has changed
onvolumechange [5]	Volume value change, or when volume is muted
onwaiting [5]	Playing is temporarily suspended

CSS Basics

'CSS' stands for *Cascading Style Sheets*. Cascading Style Sheets are similar to style sheets found in word processing and page layout application programs.

- CSS is not part of HTML but rather a stand alone standard language.
- CSS attributes and values can be manipulated by JavaScript.
- Some browser offer browser specific properties.
- CSS comments are used to add notes to the code. A CSS comment is denoted by (**/***) and (***/**) signs. Comments placed between these signs are not rendered by browsers.
- CSS can be applied as a predefined universal *rule* or as *inline* HTML attribute specific to a single HTML element.
- A style, applied to HTML element via HTML 'style' property also called an *inline style*. Inline style can control one HTML element at a time.
- A rule can be reusable: it can control multiple HTML elements.

Anatomy of a CSS Rule

A CSS rule includes HTML selector and CSS declaration.

	HTML tag, Class, or ID	CSS Declaration
Syntax concept	selector	{property: attribute;}
This book's syntax model	div	height = <u>auto</u> | <length> | inherit
Code example	**div**	**{height: 100px;}**

Typical CSS property locations

- In most cases the external CSS is a preferred way since this way one set of rules can control multiple HTML elements and multiple HTML documents.

- HTML comment tags (`<!--    -->`) may be used to hide CSS from incompatible browsers.

Location	Method of CSS Rule Declaration	Example

External CSS file	Embedded rule definition via the \<link\> HTML tag	`<head>`
		
		`<link href=styles.css rel=stylesheet type=text/css>`
		
		`</head>`

External CSS file	Embedded rule definition via the **@import** CSS declaration into:
	
	■ **\<head\>** of the document
	■ another CSS file. This allows for nesting of multiple CSS files
		`<head>`
		
		`<style type=text/css>`
		
		`<!--`
		
		`@import url(styles.css);`
		
		`-->`
		
		`</style>`
		
		`</head>`

\<head\> of the HTML document	Embedded rule definition via the **\<style\>** tag	`<head>`
		
		`<style type=text/css media=all>`
		
		`<!--`
		
		`.style1 {color:#eeeeee;}`
		
		`-->`
		
		`</style>`
		
		`</head>`

HTML element	Inline HTML 'style' attribute within the **\<body\>** of HTML document
	
	Tip: the style attribute needs no quotes as long as the values are space delimited
		`<body>`
		
		`<p style=height:100%;color:blue>`
		
		`</body>`

About CSS Properties

- Multiple property values should be delimited by space.

- "Shorthand" property combines values of multiple properties in one simplified declaration. Shorthand property can be used to minimize syntax by combining several related property values into a single "super-property".

- If property is not specified, the initial default property value applies.

CSS Cascading Priority

- CSS can 'cascade': it applies properties/values in order of priority.
- A higher priority style overwrite a lower priority style.

low	Priority Type	Comment	Example
1	Browser default	Browser default value is determined by W3C initial value specifications. It has the lowest priority and can be overwritten.	`<p style=font-weight:bold>` `Sample text</p>` `<!-- The 'bold' value overwrites default browser value 'normal'-->`
2	CSS property definition in HTML document	CSS rule or CSS inline style overwrites a default browser value.	`.myclass` `{font-weight: bold;}` `<p class=myclass>text</p>`
3	Parent inheritance	If a property is not specified, it will be inherited from a parent element.	`<div style=color: blue>` `    <p>Text</p>` `</div>`
4	Rule order	Last rule declaration has a higher priority	`div {width: auto;}` `div {width: 90%;}`
5	Selector specificity	A specific contextual selector (#heading p) overwrites generic definition	`#heading p {color: blue;}` `p {color: black;}`
6	Importance	The '!important' value overwrites the previous priority types.	`.myclass {` `font-size:12px !important;}`
7	Media Type	A property definition applies to all media types, unless a property had a media-specific CSS defined.	`<style type="text/css"` `media="print">` `.mystyle {color: blue;}`
8	Inline	A style applied to an HTML element via HTML 'style' property overwrites all the previous priority types.	`<p style=font-weight: bold>` `Sample text</p>`
9	User defined	Most browsers have the accessibility feature: a capability to load a user defined CSS.	

Selector Types

Type	Description	Example Code
Universal	Defines property for any element	`* {font-family: Times;}`
HTML tag	Defines property for any specific HTML element	`div {height: 100%;}`

Class	Defines value for the 'class' attribute. 'Class' attribute can apply a common set of property values to a multiple elements of different types.	`.myclass {font-weight: bold;}`
		
		`<p class=myclass>`
		`1st paragraph</p>`
		`<p class=myclass>`
		`2nd paragraph</p>`

Id	Defines value for the 'id' attribute. 'Id' attribute can not have duplicate values within one HTML document.	`#heading {font-weight: bold;}`
		
		`<div id=heading>`
		`First Chapter</div>`

Group	Defines a common value for a multiple elements of different types	`h2, .myclass, #title` `{font-family: Arial;}`
Descendant	Defines value for a parent-child pair	`#heading p {color: blue;}`
Child	Defines property value that only affect elements that are children of other specific elements	`#heading > p {color: blue;}`

Universal Grandchild	Defines property value for the specified grandchild element:	`section * p {color: blue;}`
		`/*(p) is at least a grandchild of the (section) element. */`
		
		`section * * p {color: blue;}`
		`/*(p) is at least a great-grandchild of the (section) element. */`
		
		`section * * table * p {color: blue;}`
		`/*(p) is at least a grandchild of the (table) element given that the (table) is at least a great-grandchild of the (section). */`

Adjacent Sibling	Elements that are immediately next to each other.
	
	Not supported in IE 6.
		`h1 + h2 {font-style: italic;}`
		
		`<h1>Title</h1>`
		`<h2>Subtitle</h2>`

General Sibling	All elements that share the same parent and elements are in the same sequence, not always immediate	`h1 ~ p {font-style: italic;}`

Type	Description	Example Code
Matching Attribute	An element with that matches the attribute listed	
	■ [att]: match when the element defines the attribute ('att')	span[class=footer] {color:blue;}
	■ [att=val]: attribute value is "val"	
	■ [att~=val]: attribute whose value is a space-separated list of keywords, one of which is "val"	p[title^="right"] {color: blue;}
	■ [att | =val]: at least the part of the attribute value is "val"	p[title$="wing"] {color: red;}
	■ [att^=val]: attribute value begins with the prefix "val"	p[title*="left"]{color: gray;}
	■ [att$=val]: attribute whose value ends with the suffix "val"	<p title="right-wing"> The right-wing conspiracy.</p>
	■ [att*=val]: attribute whose value contains at least one instance of the substring "val"	

CSS Box Model

It is essential to understand the CSS *box-object model*. This model defines the key CSS layout properties and element relationship to other page elements. The box model properties are: *margin*, *background*, *border*, *padding*, *width* and *height*. Think of each web page element as being an invisible rectangle with an invisible border and an invisible outer space.

- Margin: a transparent space immediately outside the invisible box is a margin, separating an element from other elements

- Padding: a transparent space inside the invisible box but before the content, separating an element from its border and content (e.g. text)

- Border: between the padding and the margin. The border could be virtual (invisible)

- Background: combined padding and content space

- Width and Height: define content area dimensions only

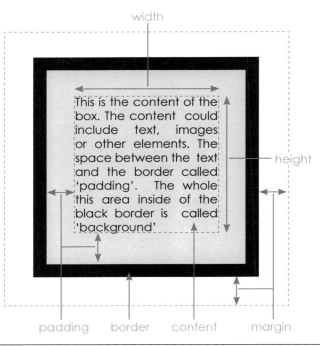

CSS Properties

Section definitions & conventions

- CSS3 specifications are still in draft mode, and could potentially change.

- In this chapter of the book, shorthand properties are formatted in bold.

- The description section has CSS properties and values delimited by single quotes.

Property model definitions & display conventions

- In this chapter of the book, a set of property values represented by a conceptual syntax 'model', which describes rules these values can be assigned.

- Syntax model section describes several types of values, using distinctive display conventions:

  - Variable data values, which are denoted by the less than (<) and greater than (>) brackets (e.g., `<image>`, `<length>`, `<color>`, etc.). Values in < > brackets are variable placeholders for actual values.

  - Variable data values, that have the same set of values wile sharing the same name as a property, appear in single quotes (e.g., `<'column-width'>`, `<'text-emphasis-style'>`, `<'background-color'>`, etc.)

  - Constant keyword values must appear literally, without any delimiting characters (e.g., normal, hidden, blue, auto, etc.). The slash (/) and the comma (,) must also appear literally.

- Pipe character (|) is a substitution for "or", meaning that values delimited by pipe character (|) generally can not be used together within a single property.

- A plus symbol (+) separates options that could be used together in any order, within a single property.

- An ampersand (&) separates values which must all occur, in any order.

- An asterisk symbol (*) indicates that the preceding value may occur zero or more times. This model example `[<URL> + [,* ]]` represents a list of multiple comma-delimited URLs. Two optional numbers in curly brackets `{X-Y}` indicate that the preceding group occurs X to Y times.

- The 'inherit' value defines whether the value is inherited from its parent. The 'inherit' value applies to every CSS property, though it is omitted from the Model row in order to simplify the content. For instance, the 'float' property model would be:
`left | right | none | inherit` . On the other hand, note that not every property has the 'inherited' quality, defining whether a property value is inherited from a parent element by default.

- In this section of the book an initial default property value is indicated by <u>underline</u>.

- In case an initial value indicator is omitted, it means initial value is not defined by standards and it is implementation dependent.

- The characters <, >, [,], |, &, +, * , and underlining are not used in CSS syntax that way, but they rather a convention of the Model row of this book.

- The ❸ symbol indicates that this is updated property or new CSS3 property.

Background

Property	Values	
background	Model	\<bg-image\> + \<bg-position\> [/ \<bg-size\>] + \<repeat-style\> + \<attachment\> + \<box\> + \<'background-color'\>
	Description	Shorthand property
	Example	`section {background:50% url('img.gif') / 8em scroll repeat-x border-box blue;}`
background-attachment	Model	scroll | fixed | local
	Description	When the page scrolls, background image: ■ scroll: fixed to the element, scrolls with the document ■ fixed: fixed with regard to the viewport ■ local: inherits element's content position, scrolls with content
	Example	`div {background-attachment: scroll;}`
background-break ❸	Model	bounding-box | continuous | each-box
	Description	Newly proposed *CSS3* property, which later was removed from the W3C Working Draft
background-clip ❸	Model	border-box | content-box | padding-box
	Description	Defines an extension of a background into a border:

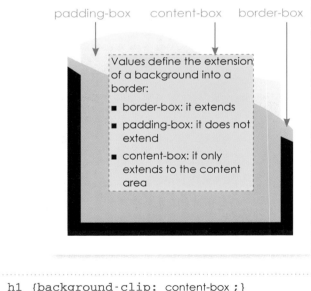

	Example	`h1 {background-clip: content-box ;}`
background-color	Model	transparent | \<color\>
	Description	Sets background color
	Example	`h1 {background-color: #F00;}`

Property	Values	
background-image ❸	Model	[<url> | <u>none</u>] + [,*]
	Description	URL defines the background image source. Box background can have multiple layers. ■ Number of layers is defined by a number of comma-delimited background-image values ■ Any value represents a layer including the value 'none' ■ Each image layer can be sized, positioned, and tiled according to the corresponding value in each of the background properties ■ The first image definition is the closest to a user ■ Example below is using the background shorthand property and PNG images saved with alpha channel transparency

	Example	`{background:url(sky.png) top left no-repeat,`
		`url(water.png) bottom left no-repeat,`
		`url(portrait.png) top   left no-repeat;}`

background-origin ❸	Model	border-box | content-box | padding-box
	Description	Defines when background position is relative to a box
	Example	`.class2 {background: url('img.jpg');` `background-origin: content-box;}`

Property	Values	
background-position	Model	[[top | bottom] | [<length%> | <lengthPixels> | left | center | right] [<length%> | <lengthPixels> | top | center | bottom] | [center | [left | right] [<length%> | <lengthPixels>] + [center | [top | bottom] [<length%> | <lengthPixels>]
	Description	■ If only one keyword, the second value will be "center" ■ The initial value is top left corner: 0 0. It could be set either by percentage or by keyword values "top left" ■ The percentages and positions could be mixed ■ Percentages refer to size of background positioning area, minus size of background image

	Example	`.class1, .class2`
		`{background-image:url(img.jpg)}`
		
		`.class1 {background-position: left top;}`
		`/* 0px, 0px */`
		
		`.class2 {background-position:`
		`left 15px top 20px;}` `/*15px, 20px */`
		
		`.class3 {background: url(img.jpg) top center}`
		`/* shorthand: 50% 0% */`

background-size	Model	[[<width > + <height>] | cover | contain
	Description	Preserving original aspect ratio to fit inside the background positioning area could be achieved by values: ■ contain: scale the image to the largest size. ■ cover: scale the image to the smallest size. The original aspect ratio could be modified by manipulating the width and height values. ■ The first value is the width, the second is the height. ■ Possible 'width' and 'height' values: [auto | pixels | %] ■ If the second value is absent, it is implied to be 'auto'. ■ In this example the image is stretched to fit horizontally 4 times. The aspect ratio is fixed:
	Example	`.class1 {background-size: 25% auto;}`

Property	Values	
background-repeat	Model	repeat-x | repeat-y | [repeat] | space | round | no-repeat]
	Description	Background repeat behavior: ■ repeat: Vertically and horizontally ■ repeat-x: Horizontally only ■ repeat-y: Vertically only ■ no-repeat: Displayed only once ■ round: Repeated as much as needed to fit within the background area. If it doesn't fit a whole number of times, it will be scaled to fit. ■ space: Repeated as often as will fit within the background positioning area to avoid clipping, and then the images will be spaced out to fill the area. First and last images touch the edges of the area: 
	Example	`body {background-repeat: space;` `background-image: url(sculpture.png) white;}`

Border

Property	Values	
border	Model	<border-width> + <border-style> + <color>
	Description	Shorthand property
	Example	`.class1 {border: 1px solid blue;}`
border-color	Model	<u><color></u>
	Description	Defines one common color for all 4 borders
	Example	`.class1 {border-color:#003333;}`

Property	Values	
border-top-color border-right-color border-bottom-color border-left-color	Model	<color>
	Description	Defines individual color for each of 4 optional borders
	Example	`.class1 {border-top-color:#003333;` `            border-right-color: blue;}`
border-style	Model	none | hidden | dotted | dashed | solid | double | groove | ridge | inset | outset
	Description	Defines one common style for all 4 borders
	Example	`.class1 {border-style: solid;}`
border-top-style border-right-style border-bottom-style border-left-style	Model	none | hidden | dotted | dashed | solid | double | groove | ridge | inset | outset
	Description	Defines individual style for each of 4 optional borders
	Example	`.class1 {border-top-style: dashed;` `            border-left-style: solid;}`
border-width	Model	<numeric> | thin | medium | thick
	Description	Defines one common width for all 4 borders. Numeric can be in pixels, points or em.
	Example	`.class1 {border-width: 1.6em;}`
border-top-width border-right-width border-bottom-width border-left-width	Model	<numeric_fixed> | thin | medium | thick
	Description	Defines individual width for each of 4 optional borders. Numeric can be in pixels, points or em.
	Example	`.class1 {border-top-width: thin;` `            border-left-width: 2px;}`
border-radius ❸	Model	[<radius_fixed> | <radius_%>] + [* 1,4]
	Description	Shorthand. Defines one common radius for all 4 corners. Fixed value can be in pixels, points or em:

	Example	`.class1 {border: solid black 6px;`
		`            border-left-width: 14px;`
		`            border-radius: 20%/40px;}`

Property	Values	
border-top-left-radius ❸ border-top-right-radius border-bottom-right-radius border-bottom-left-radius	Model	[<radius_fixed> | <radius_%>] [< radius_fixed> | <radius_%>]
	Description	Defines individual radius for each of 4 corners. Fixed value can be in pixels, points or em.
	Example	```.class1 {
border-top-left-radius: 10px 20% 1em;
border-top-right-radius: 10px 20%;}```
border-top	Model	<border-width> + <border-style> + <color>
border-right	Description	Shorthand properties
border-bottom **border-left**	Example	```.class1 {border-top: 2px solid red;
border-right: 2px dashed blue;
border-bottom: solid red;
border-left: 2px dashed blue;}```
border-collapse	Model	collapse | separate
	Description	Adjacent table cells: ■ collapsed: share borders ■ separated: each have their own borders
	Example	```table {border-collapse: collapse;}```

Border Effects

Property	Values	
border-image ❸	Model	<'border-image-source'> + <'border-image-slice'> [/<'border-image-width'>? [/<'border-image-outset'>]?] ? + <'border-image-repeat'>
	Description	Shorthand property. Defines an image to overwrite border styles specified by the 'border-style' properties and it creates an additional background layer.
	Example	

```
border: solid 50px;
border-image:url(images/flower.png) 35 repeat
stretch;
-webkit-border-image:url(images/flower.png) 35
repeat stretch;
-moz-border-image:url(images/flower.png) 35
repeat stretch;
```

Property	Values	
border-image-source ❸	Model	none	<image>
	Description	Defines an image to overwrite border styles specified by the 'border-style' properties and it creates an additional background layer
border-image-slice ❸	Model	[[<number_pixels>	<number_%>] + [*1,4]] + fill
	Description	Initial value: **100%**. Four values represent inward offsets from the top, right, bottom, and left edges of the image, dividing it into nine regions: four corners, four edges and a middle. The middle image part is discarded (treated as transparent) unless the 'fill' keyword is present. ■ <number_%>: relative to the size of the image. ■ <number_pixels>: pixels in a bitmap image or vector coordinates in a vector image. ■ Optional 'fill' keyword preserves the middle part of the border-image.
	Example	`border-image-slice:25% 30% 12% 20% fill;`
border-image-width ❸	Model	[<number_pixels>	<number_%>	<number_integer>	auto]
	Description	Initial value: '1'. Definition of the border image is drawn inside an area called the border image area. The four values of 'border-image-width' specify offsets dividing the border image area into nine parts: distances from the top, right, bottom, and left sides of the area. ■ <number_%>: the size of the border image area: the width for horizontal offsets, the height for vertical offsets. ■ <number_integer>: multiples of the corresponding 'border-width'. ■ auto: border image width is the original width or height of the corresponding image slice.
	Example	`.class1 {border-image-width: 2;}`
border-image-outset ❸	Model	[<length_pix>	<number_integer>]
	Description	■ <length_pix>: initial value: '0'. Top, right, bottom, left value of the border image area beyond the border box. ■ <number_integer>: multiples of the corresponding 'border-width'.
	Example	`.class1 {border-image-outset: 0 1em;}`

Property	Values	
border-image-repeat ❸	Model	<u>stretch</u> | repeat | round | space
	Description	Border image scaling methods: ■ stretch: stretched to fill the area. ■ repeat: tiled (repeated) to fill the area. ■ round: tiled to fill the area. If it does not fit the area with a whole number of tiles, the image is re-scaled. ■ space: tiled to fill the area. If it does not fit the area with a whole number of tiles, a space is added between the tiles.
	Example	style="border-image-repeat: round;"
box-decoration-break ❸	Model	<u>slice</u> | clone
	Description	Border and padding method at the column/line break: ■ clone: independent border and padding for each box ■ slice: one common border and padding for both boxes
box-shadow ❸	Model	<u>none</u> | [inset & [<offset-x> <offset-y> <blur-radius> <spread-radius> <color>]]
	Description	■ inset: optional keyword which defines an inner shadow ■ <offset-x>: horizontal shadow offset ■ <offset-y>: vertical shadow offset ■ <blur-radius>: shadow edge softness. 0 is sharp ■ The -webkit prefix: Safari and Chrome compatibility ■ The -moz prefix: Firefox compatibility **Box Shadow**
	Example 1	```.class1 {border:1px solid blue;` `background-color: #FFFF00;` `width: 120px; height: 120px;` `box-shadow: 10px 10px 20px 0px gray;` `-webkit-box-shadow: 10px 10px 20px 0px gray;` `-moz-box-shadow: 10px 10px 20px 0px gray;}```
	Example 2	```/* since box-shadow property is incompatible` `with most of Internet Explorer versions,` `this IE-specific alternative could be used*/`  `.class1 { filter:` `progid:DXImageTransform.Microsoft.Shadow` `(color=#C6CDD5,direction=90,strength=4)` `progid:DXImageTransform.Microsoft.Shadow` `(color=#C6CDD5,direction=180,strength=4)}```

Font

Property	Values	
font-size-adjust	Model	none	<number>
	Description	Inherited. Preserving the readability by maintaining the 'aspect value' of lowercase letters vs. their uppercase counterparts and adjusting the font-size so that the x-height is the fixed regardless of the font used. 'Aspect value' = font x-height / font size
	Example	.class1 {font-size-adjust: 0.5;}
font-stretch	Model	normal	wider	narrower	ultra-condensed	condensed	extra-condensed	semi-condensed	semi-expanded	expanded	extra-expanded	ultra-expanded
	Description	Inherited
	Example	.class1 {font-style: italic;}
font ❸	Model	[[<'font-style'> + <'font-variant'> + <'font-weight'>] <'font-size'> [/ <'line-height'>] <'font-family'>]	caption	icon	menu	message-box	small-caption	status-bar	<appearance>
	Description	Shorthand property for setting 'font-style', 'font-variant', 'font-weight', 'font-size', 'line-height' and 'font-family' properties. Inherited. The second property function is to control system font values, used for: ■ caption: captioned controls: buttons, drop-downs, etc. ■ icon: labeling icons ■ menu: drop down menus and menu lists ■ message-box: dialog boxes. ■ small-caption: small control labels ■ status-bar: window status bars ■ <appearance>: CSS3 adds the list of <appearance> values to allow system controls text styling: icon, window, desktop, workspace, document, tooltip, status-bar, dialog, message-box, button, caption, small-caption, push-button, hyperlink, radio-button, checkbox, menu-item, tab, menu, menubar, pull-down-menu, pop-up-menu, list-menu, radio-group, checkbox-group, outline-tree, range, field, combo-box, signature, password
	Example	.class1 {font: x-large/1.5em "Palatino", serif;} button p {font: menu;}
font-family	Model	[<family-name>	<generic-family>] + [, *]
	Description	Inherited
	Example	p {font-family: Arial, Gill, sans-serif;}

Property	Values	
font-size	Model	\<absolute-size> | \<relative-size> | \<numeric_fixed> | \<numeric_%>
	Description	Inherited ■ \<absolute-size> values: [xx-small | x-small | small | medium | large | x-large | xx-large] ■ \<relative-size> values: [larger | smaller]
	Example	`.class1 {font-size: 12px;}` `/*numeric_fixed*/`
font-weight	Model	100 | 200 | 300 | 400 | 500 | 600 | 700 | 800 | 900 | bold | bolder | lighter | normal
	Description	Inherited
	Example	`.class1 {font-weight: bold;}`

Box Model

Property	Values	
clear	Model	none | left | right | both
	Description	Side of an element where other floating elements will not be allowed ■ left: no floating elements allowed on the left ■ right: no floating elements allowed on the right ■ both: no floating elements allowed on either side ■ none: allows floating elements on both sides
	Example	`.class1 {clear: left;}`
display	Model	inline | block | inline-block | list-item | run-in | compact | table | inline-table | table-row-group | table-header-group | table-footer-group | table-row | table-column-group | none | table-column | table-cell | table-caption | ruby | ruby-base | ruby-text | ruby-base-group | ruby-text-group | \<template>
	Description	Element display method. Element is displayed as: ■ block: block / paragraph. Block allows no HTML elements next to it, except when a float property assigned to another element. ■ inline: on the line of the current block ■ list-item: block box and a list-item in-line box ■ none: block is not created ■ run-in: either block or in-line boxes, depending on context ■ table, inline-table, table-row-group, table-column, table-column-group, table-header-group, table-footer-group, table-row, table-cell, and table-caption: these values define table-style element behavior
	Example	`.class1 {display: inline;}`

Property	Values	
float	Model	left | right | <u>none</u>
	Description	This property defines box floating method/direction. The property does not apply to elements that are absolutely positioned.
	Example	`.class1 {float: right;}`
height width	Model	<u>auto</u> | <length_fixed> | <length_%>
	Description	Defines height and width of an element
	Example	`.class1 {width: 12px; height: 50%;}`
max-height max-width min-height min-width	Model	<u>auto</u> | <length_fixed> | <length_%>
	Description	Defines maximum or minimum height and width of an element.
	Example	`.class1 {font-size: 12px;}`
margin	Model	<margin-top> + <margin-right> + <margin-bottom> + <margin-left>
	Description	Shorthand property. Margin defines transparent space around elements, outside of the border. It can have from 1 to 4 values.

	Example	`.class1 {margin: inherit 0 10%;}`
		`/* top:inherit;left & right:0, bottom:10%*/`
		
		`.class2 {margin: auto;}`
		`/* top, left, bottom, right: auto */`
		
		`.class3 {margin: 15px 10px;}`
		`/* top & bottom:15px; left & right:10px */`

margin-bottom margin-left margin-right margin-top	Model	<width_numeric> | auto
	Description	■ Initial value: 0 ■ Acceptable 'width_numeric' units: [px | pt | % | em]
	Example	`.class1 {margin-top: 8%;}`
padding	Model	<padding-top> + <padding-right> + <padding-bottom> + <padding-left>
	Description	Shorthand property. Padding defines space around content, inside of the element border. It can have from 1 to 4 values.

	Example	`.class1 {padding: inherit 0 10%;}`
		`/* top:inherit; left & right:0, bottom:10% */`
		
		`.class2 {padding: 15px;}`
		`/* top, left, bottom, right: 15px */`
		
		`.class3 {padding: 15px 10px;}`
		`/* top & bottom:15px; left & right:10px */`

Property	Values	
padding-bottom padding-left padding-right padding-top	Model	`<width_numeric>`
	Description	▪ Initial value: **0** ▪ Acceptable `<width_numeric>` units: [px | pt | % | em]
	Example	`.class1 {padding-top: 8%;}`
overflow	Model	[visible | hidden | scroll | auto | no-display | no-content] + [visible | hidden | scroll | auto | no-display | no-content]
	Description	▪ Shorthand for 'overflow-x' and 'overflow-y' properties. ▪ The second property value is optional. If it has one value, it defines both 'overflow-x' and 'overflow-y'.
	Example	`.class1 {overflow: scroll auto;}` `/* overflow-x = scroll; overflow-y = auto*/`
overflow-style ❸	Model	<u>auto</u> | marquee-line | marquee-block
	Description	Inherited. Defines the 'overflow' property scrolling method. ▪ auto: browser chooses the scrolling method and displays a scroll bar when it detects the clipped content. ▪ marquee-line: the content is clipped to the left and right of the box. The content scrolls horizontally. ▪ marquee-block: the content is clipped above and below the box. The content scrolls vertically.
	Example	`.class1 {overflow-style: marquee-block;}`
overflow-x ❸ overflow-y ❸	Model	<u>visible</u> | hidden | scroll | auto | no-display | no-content
	Description	▪ visible: the content is not clipped, but partially hidden. ▪ hidden: the content is clipped and no scrolling is available. ▪ scroll: the content is clipped and the scrolling is always on. ▪ auto: browser chooses the scrolling method and displays a scroll bar when it detects the clipped content. ▪ no-display: if the content doesn't fit in the box, the box is not displayed, as if 'display: none' is set. ▪ no-content: if the content doesn't fit in the box, the content is hidden, as if 'visibility: hidden' is set.
	Example	`.class1 {overflow-x: scroll;}`
rotation ❸	Model	`<angle>`
	Description	Box rotation angle. Initial value: **0**.
	Example	`.class1 {rotation: 45deg;}`

Property	Values	
rotation-point ❸	Model	<bg-position>
	Description	Initial value: `50% 50%`.
	Example	`.class1 {rotation-point: top left;}`
visibility	Model	visible | hidden | collapse
	Description	Inherited. This property specifies whether the boxes generated by an element are rendered. Invisible boxes still affect layout unless the 'display' is 'none'. ■ visible: the box is visible. ■ hidden: the box is hidden, but still it affects layout by taking up the same space. ■ collapse: it applies for internal table objects: rows, row groups, columns, and column groups (the same effect as 'hidden').
	Example	`.class1 {visibility: hidden;}`

Marquee

Property	Values	
marquee-direction ❸	Model	forward | reverse
	Description	Inherited. Defines the initial direction of the marquee effect. ■ forward: hidden text appears in the normal reading order. ■ reverse: hidden text appears in reverse reading order.
	Example	`.class1 {marquee-direction: reverse;}`
marquee-play-count ❸	Model	<non-negative-integer> | infinite
	Description	Formerly it was called 'marquee-loop'. Initial value: 1. Frequency of the moving the content
	Example	`.class1 {marquee-play-count: 2;}`
marquee-speed ❸	Model	slow | normal | fast
	Description	Marquee animation speed
	Example	`.class1 {marquee-speed: slow;}`
marquee-style ❸	Model	scroll | slide | alternate
	Description	■ scroll: start hidden, scroll all the way across and hide completely off. ■ slide: start completely hidden, scroll in, then the content stops moving once the last content is visible. ■ alternate: the content moves back and forth within the box in the direction specified by 'marquee-direction' property.
	Example	`.class1 {marquee-style: slide;}`

Text Formatting

Property	Values	
direction	Model	ltr	rtl
	Description	Text direction. ■ ltr: left-to-right. ■ rtl: right-to-left: useful for some languages, such as Hebrew.
	Example	`.class1 {direction: rtl;}`
hanging-punctuation ❸	Model	none	[start + end + end-edge]
	Description	Inherited. Punctuation mark positioning: ■ start: outside the start edge of the first line. ■ end: outside the end edge of the last line. ■ end-edge: outside the end edge of all lines.
	Example	`.class1 {hanging-punctuation: 2;}`
letter-spacing	Model	normal	<length_Fixed>	<length_%>
word-spacing	Description	Inherited. Defines space between letters / words.
	Example	`.class1 {letter-spacing: 0.5em;}`
punctuation-trim ❸	Model	none	[start + adjacent + end]
	Description	Trimming (kerning) method for the blank half of a 'full character width' punctuation character: ■ none: no trimming. ■ start: trim the opening punctuation at the beginning of line. ■ end: trim the closing punctuation at the end of each line. ■ adjacent: trim the opening/closing punctuation if is adjacent to another opening/closing punctuation.
	Example	`p {punctuation-trim: start adjacent end;}`
text-align ❸	Model	start	end	left	right	center	justify	<text_string>
	Description	Inherited. In-line content horizontal alignment to: ■ left: left edge of the line. ■ right: right edge of the line. ■ center: centered within the line. ■ justify: text is justified. New values in *CSS3*: ■ start: start edge of the line. ■ end: end edge of the line. ■ <string>: table cell alignment using text string as reference. The code example below aligns on the decimal period.
	Example	`.class1 {text-align: . ;}`

Property	Values	
text-align-last ➌	Model	<u>start</u> | end | left | right | center | justify
	Description	Inherited. Defines alignment for the last or only line of text.
	Example	`.class1 {text-align: end;}`
text-justify ➌	Model	<u>auto</u> | [trim + [inter-word | inter-ideograph | inter-cluster | distribute | kashida]]
	Description	Inherited. Defines justification method used when **text-align** property is set to 'justify'. ■ auto: browser-defined. ■ inter-word: defines spacing between words. ■ inter-ideograph: defines spacing between characters in Chinese, Japanese and Korean languages that use no word spaces. If Latin characters are also present in-line, they are not be affected. ■ inter-cluster: defines spacing between characters in Southeast Asian languages which don't use spaces between words, such as Thai and Lao. ■ distribute: defines spacing between both words and characters. ■ kashida: defines spacing in Arabic and related scripts through the use of *kashida*. In contrast to white-space justification, kashida justification is achieved by stretching characters. ■ trim: applies the blank space trimming instead of expansion.
	Example	`.class1 {text-justify:  inter-cluster;}`
text-decoration ➌	Model	<text-decoration-line> + <text-decoration-color> + <text-decoration-style> + blink
	Description	Shorthand property. The omitted 'text-decoration-color' and 'text-decoration-style' values are backwards-compatible with CSS 2.1.

	Example	`.class1`
		`{text-decoration: underline;`
		`/* compatible with both CSS3 and CSS2.1 */`
		
		`text-decoration: green dotted underline;}`
		`/* ignored in CSS2.1 */`

text-emphasis ➌	Model	<'text-emphasis-style'> + <'text-emphasis-color'>
	Description	Shorthand property. Inherited.
	Example	`.class1 {text-emphasis: filled #000000;}`

Property	Values	
text-indent ❸	Model	[[<u><length_fixed></u> | <length_%>] + [hanging + each-line]]
	Description	Initial value **0**. Inherited.
		Indent is a margin applied to the first line of the text block.
		■ <length_fixed>: absolute margin value (e.g. px, pt)
		■ <length_%>: relative margin value (e.g. %)
		■ each-line: indentation affects every line in the paragraph
		■ hanging: no indentation on the 1st line
	Example	`.class1 {text-indent: 5px hanging;}`
text-outline ❸	Model	<u>none</u> | [<color> <length> <length> | <length> <length> <color>]
	Description	Inherited. The first length represents the outline's thickness and the second represents an optional blur radius.
	Example	`.class1 {text-outline: 2px 3px red;}`
text-shadow ❸	Model	<u>none</u> | [[<shadow>] + [,*]]
	Description	Inherited. List of multiple comma-separated shadow effects could be defined. The <shadow> value matches the 'box-shadow' property values definitions, with the exception of the 'inset' keyword.
		Text Shadow
	Example	`.class1 {text-shadow: 3px 3px 3px gray;}`
text-transform ❸	Model	<u>none</u> | capitalize | uppercase | lowercase | fullwidth | large-kana
	Description	Inherited.
		■ capitalize: title-case, every word starts with capital letter.
		■ uppercase: capital letters
		■ lowercase: lower-case
		■ fullwidth: all characters are in full-width form
		■ large-kana: small-to-large Kana character conversion
	Example	`.class1 {text-transform: uppercase;}`
text-wrap ❸	Model	<u>normal</u> | unrestricted | none | suppress
	Description	Inherited. Text wrapping method definition:
		■ normal: regular text wrapping.
		■ none: no wrapping, which is normally a cause of overflow.
		■ unrestricted: line may break between any two characters. This could be useful for an Asian script (e.g. Chinese).
		■ suppress: line breaking is suppressed within the element, except when there are no other valid break points.
	Example	`.class1 {text-wrap: unrestricted;}`

Property	Values	
unicode-bidi	Model	<u>normal</u> | embed | bidi-override
	Description	Formatting definition of the *bi-directional* flow of content based on controls for language "embeddings" and directional overrides. The property determines the method of mapping to the Unicode algorithm. ■ normal: no additional level of embedding. ■ embed: additional level of embedding is opened and it is given by the direction property. ■ bidi-override: override for inline-level elements.
	Example	`.class1 {unicode-bidi: embed;}`
white-space ❸	Model	<u>normal</u> | pre | nowrap | pre-wrap | pre-line
	Description	Inherited. Shorthand for the 'white-space-collapsing' and 'text-wrap' properties. Not all combinations are represented. ■ normal: white-space-collapsing:collapse; text-wrap:normal; ■ pre: white-space-collapsing: preserve; text-wrap:none; ■ nowrap: white-space-collapsing:collapse; text-wrap:none; ■ pre-wrap: white-space-collapsing:preserve; text-wrap:normal; ■ pre-line: white-space-collapsing:preserve-breaks; text-wrap:normal;
	Example	`.class1 {white-space: pre-wrap;}`
white-space-collapsing ❸	Model	<u>collapse</u> | discard | [[preserve | preserve-breaks] &trim-inner]
	Description	Inherited. This property is still in draft mode. It could be potentially renamed to 'white-space-trim' or 'white-space-adjust'. The white-space processing rules definitions: ■ collapse: collapsing of white-spaces into a single character. ■ preserve: collapsing of white-spaces is prevented. Segment breaks are preserved as forced line breaks. ■ preserve-breaks: collapsing of white-spaces, while segment breaks are preserved as forced line breaks. ■ discard: all white-space in the element is discarded. ■ trim-inner: discarding white-space at the beginning of a block up to the last line break, before the first non-white-space character in the block, as well as discarding white-space at the end of a block starting with the first line break after the last non-white-space character in the block.
	Example	`.class1 {white-space-collapsing: discard;}`

Property	Values	
word-break ❸	Model	<u>normal</u> | break-all | hyphenate
	Description	Inherited. Useful if multiple languages are present within an element. Non-CJK (Chinese, Japanese, Korean) word-break could be controlled separately. ■ break-all: break between any 2 characters for non-CJK scripts ■ hyphenate: words may be broken at certain places based on hyphenation rules for given language Values under consideration: 'hyphenate-all' and 'none'.
	Example	`.class1 {word-break: break-all;}`
word-spacing ❸ letter-spacing ❸	Model	<length-limit-min> + <length-limit-opt> + <length-limit-max>
	Description	Inherited. Minimum, maximum, and optimal spacing between words. The acceptable units: [<em> | normal | <%>]
	Example	`.class1 {word-spacing: 0.2em  normal  3%;}`
word-wrap ❸	Model	<u>normal</u> | break-word
	Description	Inherited. Defines break within a word to prevent overflow. ■ normal: regular line-break behavior ■ break-word: a word may be broken at any point
	Example	`.class1 {word-wrap: break-word;}`

Color

Property	Values	
color ❸	Model	<color> | attr(X,color)
	Description	Inherited ■ <color>: a keyword or a numerical RGB value. See Appendix for the list of keyword values. ■ attr(X,color): the function returns color as value of attribute X
	Example	`h1 {color: rgb(240,6,10);}`
opacity ❸	Model	<alphavalue>
	Description	Values range between **0.0** (transparent) to initial value **1.0** (opaque) Tip: RGBA declaration allows you to set opacity via the Alpha channel, as part of the color value **rgba(255,0,0,0.5)**

	Example	`.class1 {opacity: 0.5;}`
		
		`.class2 {background-color: rgba(255,0,0,0.5);}`

Property	Values	
color-profile ❸	Model	auto | sRGB | <URL>
	Description	Inherited
	Example	.class1 {color-profile: "http://www.colors.corp/ images/profiles/mah314.icm"}
rendering-intent ❸	Model	auto | perceptual | relative-colorimetric | saturation | absolute-colorimetric
	Description	Inherited. All the values other than 'auto' are standardized by the International Color Consortium.
	Example	.class1 {rendering-intent:saturation;}

Multi-column and Grid layout

Property	Values	
break-after ❸ break-before ❸	Model	<u>auto</u> | always | avoid | left | right | page | column | avoid-page | avoid-column
	Description	Column break method for the multiple column layout: ■ auto: neither force nor forbid a page/column break ■ always: force page break ■ avoid: avoid a page/column break ■ left: force 1 or 2 page breaks to format the next page as a left page ■ right: force 1 or 2 page breaks to format the next page as a right page ■ page: force page break ■ column: force a column break ■ avoid-page: avoid a page break ■ avoid-column: avoid a column break
	Example	.class1 {break-after: avoid-page;}
break-inside	Model	<u>auto</u> | avoid | avoid-page | avoid-column
column-count ❸	Model	<integer_number> | <u>auto</u>
	Description	Number of columns definition ■ auto: value determined by other properties, such as 'column-width' ■ <integer>: a numeric value
	Example	.class1 {column-count: 3;}

Property	Values	
column-width ❸	Model	\<length\> | <u>auto</u>
	Description	Columns width definition. ■ auto: value determined by other properties, such as 'column-count' ■ \<length\>: a numeric value
	Example	`.class1 {column-width: 3.5em;}`
columns ❸	Model	<'column-width'> + <'column-count'>
	Description	Shorthand property
	Example	`.class1 {column-width:90px; column-count:2;}`
column-fill ❸	Model	auto | <u>balance</u>
	Description	■ balance: content is equally balanced between columns ■ auto: sequential fill
	Example	`div {column-fill: balance;}`
column-gap	Model	\<length\> | <u>normal</u>
	Description	Gap (space, gutter) between columns.
	Example	`.class1 {column-gap: 1em;}`
column-rule ❸	Model	\<column-rule-width\> + \<border-style\> + [\<color\> | transparent]
	Description	Shorthand property
	Example	`.class1 {column-rule: 2px dotted blue;}`
column-rule-color ❸	Model	\<color\>
	Description	Initial value depends on browser.
	Example	`.class1 {column-rule-color: black;}`
column-rule-style ❸	Model	<'border-style'>
	Description	Based on the 'border-style' property. Values: none | hidden | dotted | dashed | solid | double | groove | ridge | inset | outset
	Example	`.class1 {column-rule-style: dotted;}`
column-rule-width ❸	Model	<'border-width'>
	Description	Initial value: **medium**. Based on the 'border-width' property. Valid values: \<numeric\> | thin | medium | thick
	Example	`.class1 {column-rule-width: 3px;}`

Property	Values	
column-span ❸	Model	1	all
	Description	Defines the number of columns. ■ 1: no span across columns ■ all: span across all columns
	Example	.class1 {column-span: 1;}
column-width ❸	Model	<length>	auto
	Example	.class1 {column-width: 50px;}
grid-columns ❸ grid-rows	Model	[[<length>	<percentage>	<relative_length>] | ([<length> | <percentage> | <relative_length >]) ['['<integer>']'] ?]	none
	Description	Defines grid-based layout, similar to the grids traditionally used in magazines and newspapers.
	Example	.class1 {grid-columns: * * (0.7in * *) [2]; grid-rows:25% *; columns:3; column-gap:0.7in;} .class2 {grid-rows: 3em (0.5em 1.2em); grid-columns: * (1.2em *) [2];}

Flexible Box Layout

Property	Values	
box-align ❸	Model	start	end	center	baseline	stretch
	Description	Box content alignment across (perpendicular to) the direction of its layout ■ start: normally, the top of the box ■ end: the bottom of the box ■ center: the center of the box ■ baseline: baseline-aligned, if the box orientation is 'inline-axis' or 'horizontal'. The baseline is interpreted as center, if the box orientation is 'block-axis' or 'vertical' ■ stretch: the height of the content is scaled to match the containing box
	Example	div {box-align: baseline;}

Property	Values	
box-direction ❸	Model	normal	reverse

	Description	Based on the value of the 'box-orient' property, the display direction of a box content:
		■ normal:
		  - left-to-right, if the 'box-orient' property value is 'horizontal'
		  - top-to-bottom, if the 'box-orient' property value is 'vertical'
		■ reverse: right-to-left or bottom-to-top.

	Example	`.class1 {box-direction: reverse;}`
box-flex ❸	Model	<number>
	Description	Initial value: `0.0`. ■ Defines if an elements within a box is flexible. Flexible element would be scaled automatically while filling the inner space of the containing box, if the space becomes available. Inflexible elements do not scale. ■ The flexible element is only scaled in the axis along the box's orientation. For instance, the width is affected in a horizontal box, or height in a vertical box.
	Example	`.class1 {box-flex: 0.5;}`
box-flex-group ❸	Model	<integer>
	Description	Initial value: `1`. Defines if a group of elements within a box is flexible
	Example	`.class1 {box-flex-group: 2;}`
box-lines ❸	Model	single	multiple
	Description	■ single: typically the horizontal box content will be placed in a single row, and the vertical box content will be placed in a single column. ■ multiple: allows for a multiple rows/columns.
	Example	`.class1 {box-lines: multiple;}`
box-ordinal-group ❸	Model	<integer>
	Description	Initial value: `1`. Ordinal group allows to define the order in which the elements will appear
	Example	`.class1 {box-ordinal-group: 3;}`

Property	Values		
box-orient ❸	Model	horizontal | vertical | <u>inline-axis</u> | block-axis	
	Description	Method of a content orientation within the box. ■ horizontal: left-to-right ■ vertical: top-to-bottom ■ inline-axis: along the in-line axis ■ block-axis: along the block axis	
	Example	`.class1 {box-orient: vertical;}`	
box-pack ❸	Model	<u>start</u> | end | center | justify	
	Description	Defines the method: an additional space is distributed between elements within its parent box. ■ start: the first element starts on the left edge, while all the extra space appears after the last element. ■ end: the last element starts on the right edge, while all the extra space appears before the first element. For the reverse direction boxes, the behavior is reversed. ■ center: the extra space is divided evenly, (e.g. the space gap before the first element and the gap after the last element are equal). ■ justify: the extra space is divided evenly in-between each element, while no extra space is added before the first element and after the last element.	
	Example	`.class1 {box-pack: end;}`	
box-sizing ❸	Model	<u>content-box</u> | border-box	
	Description	Method of altering the default CSS box model respectively of widths and heights of an element. ■ content-box: the box sizes apply to the content only (W3C / CSS2.1 model). ■ border-box: the box sizes apply to the border and everything inside it (traditional model).	
	Example	`.class1 {box-sizing: border-box;}`	

Speech

Property	Values	
voice-volume ❸	Model	\<number> | \<percentage> | silent | x-soft | soft | <u>medium</u> | loud | x-loud
	Description	Inherited. ■ \<number>: '**0**' to '**100**' integer or floating point number ■ \<percentage>: relative to the inherited value ■ silent | x-soft | soft | medium | loud | x-loud: non-variable fixed volume levels - 'silent' is mapped to '**0**' - 'x-loud' is mapped to '**100**'. - mapping of other values may vary
	Example	`.class1 {voice-volume: x-loud;}`
voice-balance ❸	Model	\<number> | left | <u>center</u> | right | leftwards | rightwards
	Description	Inherited. Defines the balance between left and right stereo channels: ■ \<number>: '**0**' to '**100**' integer or floating point number - '**-100**': only left channel is audible - '**100**' | '**+100**': only the right channel is audible - '**0**': both channels have the same level ■ left: equal to '**-100**' ■ center: equal to '**0**' ■ right: equal to '**100**' | '**+100**' ■ leftwards: shifts the sound to the left ■ rightwards: shifts the sound to the right
	Example	`.class1 {voice-balance: -45.5;}`
speak ❸	Model	none | <u>normal</u> | spell-out | digits | literal-punctuation | no-punctuation
	Description	Inherited. Defines the method of text rendered aurally: ■ none: no aural rendering ■ normal: language-dependent pronunciation rendered naturally with pauses. ■ spell-out: spells the text one letter at a time ■ digits: speak numbers one digit at a time ■ literal-punctuation: similar to 'normal' value, but punctuation to be spoken literally ■ no-punctuation: similar to 'normal' value but punctuation is not to be spoken literally nor rendered as pauses
	Example	`.class1 {speak: literal-punctuation;}`

Property	Values	
pause-before ❸	Model	<time> | none | x-weak | weak | medium | strong | x-strong
pause-after	Description	Initial value vary. Pause timing and rest/prosodic boundary definitions.
rest-before ❸		■ <time>: seconds and milliseconds, e.g. '5s' or '120ms'
rest-after		■ none, x-weak, weak, medium, strong, and x-strong: prosodic strength of the break in speech output
	Example	.class1 {pause-before: medium;}
cue-before ❸	Model	<URL> [<number> | <percentage> | silent | x-soft | soft | medium | loud | x-loud] | none
cue-after	Description	Sounds to be played before or after the element to delimit it.
		■ <URL>: auditory icon resource.
	Example	.class1 {cue-before: url(music.mp3) 20%;}
pause ❸	Model	<'pause-before'> + <'pause-after'>
	Description	Shorthand property.
	Example	.class1 {pause: none 200ms;}
rest ❸	Model	<'rest-before'> + <'rest-after'>
	Description	Shorthand property.
	Example	.class1 {rest: weak strong;}
cue ❸	Model	<'cue-before'> + <'cue-after'>
	Description	Shorthand property
mark-before ❸	Model	<text_string>
mark-after	Description	Non audible named markers can be attached to an audio stream as reference points.
	Example	.class1 {mark-before: "intro";}
mark ❸	Model	<'mark-before'> + <'mark-after'>
	Description	Shorthand property
	Example	.class1 {mark: "intro" "epilogue";}
voice-family ❸	Model	[<specific-voice> | [<age>] <generic-voice>] [<number>] + [,*]
	Description	A comma-separated list of voice family names in order of priority.
		■ <specific-voice>: specific character instances (e.g., "parking-attendant", samuel, napoleon).
		■ <age>: allowed values: 'child' | 'young' | 'old'
		■ <generic-voice>: allowed values: 'male'| 'female' | 'neutral'
		■ <integer_number>: voice availability order
	Example	.class1 {voice-family: young;}

Property	Values	
voice-rate ❸	Model	<percentage> | x-slow | slow | medium | fast | x-fast
	Description	Speaking rate definition. ■ <percentage>: 50% is one half of a normal rate. ■ x-slow, slow, medium, fast, x-fast: predefined rate values
	Example	.class1 {voice-rate: none 200ms;}
voice-pitch ❸	Model	<number> | x-low | low | medium | high | x-high
	Description	Inherited. Average voice pitch (frequency)
	Example	.class1 {voice-pitch: 50%;}
voice-pitch-range ❸	Model	<number> | <percentage> | x-low | low | medium | high | x-high
	Description	Inherited. Specifies range variation of voice frequency.
	Example	.class1 {voice-pitch-range: medium;}
voice-stress ❸	Model	strong | moderate | none | reduced
	Description	Strength of emphasis definition, based on a combination of pitch change, timing, and loudness.
	Example	.class1 {voice-stress: reduced;}
voice-duration ❸	Model	<time>
	Example	.class1 {voice-duration: 200ms;}
phonemes ❸	Model	<string>
	Description	Defines a phonetic text pronunciation.
	Example	.class1 {phonemes: "abracadabra";}

Table

Property	Values	
border-collapse	Model	collapse | separate
	Description	Inherited. ■ collapse: borders are collapsed into a single border, sharing a common border between table cells. ■ separate: each table cell has its own border.
	Example	.class1 {border-collapse: collapse;}

Property	Values	
border-spacing	Model	<length> <length>
	Description	Inherited. Distance between borders of adjacent cells if the property 'border-collapse' is set to 'separate'.
	Example	`.class1 {border-collapse: separate; border-spacing: 3px 3px;}`
caption-side	Model	<u>top</u> | bottom | left | right
	Description	Inherited. Defines table caption location
	Example	`.class1 {caption-side: bottom;}`
empty-cells	Model	<u>show</u> | hide
	Description	Inherited. Defines display mode for borders and background on empty table cells if the property 'border-collapse' is set to 'separate'.
	Example	`.class1 {empty-cells: hide;}`
table-layout	Model	<u>auto</u> | fixed
	Description	Defines the table layout algorithm: ■ auto: column width is defined by the widest unbreakable content in any row ■ fixed: column widths is determined by the cells in the first row only. Faster table rendering.
	Example	`.class1 {table-layout: fixed;}`

Auto Numbering and Lists

Property	Values	
list-style	Model	<'list-style-type'> + <'list-style-position'> + <'list-style-image'>
	Description	Shorthand property
	Example	`.class1 {list-style: lower-roman url("http://domain.com/star.gif") inside;}`
list-style-image	Model	<url> | <u>none</u>
	Description	Defines image as the list item marker
	Example	`.class1 {list-style-image: url("http://domain.com/dot.gif");}`
list-style-position	Model	inside | <u>outsides</u>
	Description	Defines if the list-item marker should appear inside or outside the content box.
	Example	`.class1 {list-style-position: inside;}`

Property	Values	
list-style-type	Model	[none | disc | circle | square] | [decimal | decimal-leading-zero | lower-roman | upper-roman | lower-greek | lower-latin | upper-latin | armenian | georgian | lower-alpha | upper-alpha]
	Description	Inherited. Styling of the list item marker. The first group represents unordered list values, and the second group - ordered list values: ■ armenian: e.g. A, B, G, D, etc. ■ decimal: decimal number, beginning with 1 ■ decimal-leading-zero: e.g. 01, 02, 03, etc. ■ georgian: Georgian numbering, e.g. an, ban, etc. ■ lower-alpha: e.g. a, b, c, d, e, etc. ■ lower-greek: e.g. alpha, beta, gamma, etc. ■ lower-latin: e.g. a, b, c, d, e, etc. ■ lower-roman: e.g. i, ii, iii, iv, etc. ■ upper-alpha: e.g. A, B, C, D etc. ■ upper-latin: e.g. A, B, C, D, etc. ■ upper-roman: I, II, III, IV, etc.
	Example	`.class1 {list-style-type: lower-alpha;}`
marker-offset	Model	auto | length
	Description	The 'marker-offset' property is obsoleted in CSS3, and it is replaced by the 'margin-end' property.

Animation and Transitions *

Property	Values	
animation ③	Model	[<animation-name> + <animation-duration> + <animation-timing-function> + <animation-delay> + <animation-iteration-count> + <animation-direction>] + [, *]
	Description	Shorthand property.
	Example	`.class1 { animation: "splash" 12s, "main" 20s, "splash" 12s alternate;}`
animation-delay ③ animation-duration	Model	[<time>] + [, *]
	Description	Initial value: **0**. Animation playback-delay and playback-duration properties
	Example	`.class1 { animation-delay:2s; animation-duration: 50s;}`

Property	Values	
animation-direction ❸	Model	[normal	alternate] + [, *]
	Description	Defines a reverse playback on alternate cycles. ■ normal: normal playback ■ alternate: reverse playback
	Example	.class1 {animation-direction: alternate;}
animation-iteration-count ❸	Model	[infinite	<number>] + [, *]
	Description	Initial Value: 1. Number of animation cycles
	Example	.class1 {animation-iteration-count: 3;}
animation-name ❸	Model	[none	<text_string>] + [, *]
	Description	■ <text_string>: defines a list of animation sequences by name, while name is related to an animation keyframe. ■ none: If the animation name is "none" then there will be no animation
	Example	.class1 {animation-name: "splash";}
animation-play-state ❸	Model	[running	paused] + [, *]
	Description	New but considered for removal from the current draft specification
animation-timing-function transition-timing-function ❸	Model	[ease	linear	ease-in	ease-out	ease-in-out	cubic-bezier(<number>, <number>, <number>, <number>)]+ [, *]
	Description	Defines the method how the intermediate animation/transition frames will be calculated: ■ cubic-bezier: four values define points P1 and P2 of the curve as (x1, y1, x2, y2). Values must be in the range [0, 1] ■ ease: equivalent to cubic-bezier(0.25, 0.1, 0.25, 1.0) ■ linear: equivalent to cubic-bezier(0.0, 0.0, 1.0, 1.0) ■ ease-in: equivalent to cubic-bezier(0.42, 0, 1.0, 1.0) ■ ease-out: equivalent to cubic-bezier(0, 0, 0.58, 1.0) ■ ease-in-out: equivalent to cubic-bezier(0.42, 0, 0.58, 1.0)
	Example	.class1 { animation-timing-function: linear, ease-in;}
transition ❸	Model	[<'transition-property'> + <'transition-duration'> + <'transition-timing-function'> + <'transition-delay'>] + [, *]
	Description	Shorthand property
	Example	.class1 {transition: opacity 2s linear;}

Property	Values		
transition-delay ❸	Model	[<time>] + [, *]	
transition-duration	Description	Initial value: **0**. Animation transition-delay and transition-duration	
	Example	`.class1 { transition-delay: 2s;` `transition-duration: 50s;}`	
transition-property ❸	Model	none | <u>all</u> | [<property_name>] + [, *]	
	Description	Defines a name of the property to which the transition is applied	
	Example	`.class1 {transition-property: opacity;}`	

*See the Appendix chapter for the list of properties which can be animated.

Outline

Property	Values		
outline	Model	<'outline-color'> + <'outline-style'> + <'outline-width'>	
	Description	Shorthand Property. Outline is similar to borders but it does not take up space and it may be non-rectangular.	
	Example	`.class1 {outline: red dashed 2px;}`	
outline-color	Model	<color> | <u>invert</u>	
	Description	The color value can be 'inverted' to display the opposite value.	
	Example	`.class1 {outline-color: red;}`	
outline-style	Model	auto | [<u>none</u> | dotted | dashed | solid | double | groove | ridge | inset | outset	
	Description	Defines one common style for all 4 borders	
	Example	`.class1 {outline-style: outset;}`	
outline-offset ❸	Model	<length>	
	Description	Initial value: **0**. Defines the outline offset beyond the border edge.	
	Example	`.class1 {outline-offset: 3px;}`	
outline-width	Model	<numeric> | thin | <u>medium</u> | thick	
	Example	`.class1 {outline-width: thin;}`	

2D and 3D Transforms

Property	Values	
backface-visibility	Model	visible	hidden
	Description	Defines the back side visibility of a transformed element.
	Example	.class1 {backface-visibility: hidden;}
perspective	Model	none	<number>
	Description	Applies the [perspective: number] transformation to the children of the element, not to the element itself.
	Example	.class1 {perspective: 2;}
perspective-origin ❸	Model	[[<length_%>	<length_fixed>	left	center	right] [<length_%>	<length_fixed>	top	center	bottom]]	[[left	center	right] + [top	center	bottom]]
	Description	Initial value: **50% 50%**. Defines **X** and **Y** position for the 'perspective' property.
	Example	.class1 {perspective-origin: left top;}
transform ❸	Model	none	[[<transform-function>] + [, *]]
	Description	Defines a list of space delimited *transform functions*. The list of transform functions available in the Appendix chapter.
	Example	.class1 {transform: rotate(40deg) scale(2.0);}
transform-origin ❸	Model	[[[<percentage>	<length>	left	center	right] [<percentage>	<length>	top	center	bottom]] <length>]	[[[left	center	right] + [top	center	bottom]] <length>]
	Description	Initial value: **50% 50% 0**. Defines the 3D origin of an element transformation
	Example	.class1 {transform-origin: left 10% top;}
transform-style ❸	Model	flat	preserve-3d
	Description	Initial value: **0**. Defines the way nested elements rendered in 3D space. ■ flat: rendering in 2D space ■ preserve-3d: rendering in 3D space
	Example	.class1 {transform-style: preserve-3d;}

CSS 'Transform' property functions

CSS Function	Description
`matrix(<number>, <number>, <number>, <number>, <number>, <number>)`	6- value matrix for 2D transformation
`matrix3d(<number>, <number>, <number>, <number>, <number>, <number>, <number>, <number>, <number>, <number>, <number>, <number>, <number>, <number>, <number>, <number>)`	16-value matrix for 3D transformation.
`translate(<translation-value> + [, <translation-value>])`	2D translation by the two vectors
`translate3d(<translation-value>, <translation-value>, <translation-value>)`	3D translation by the 3 vectors
`translateX(<translation-value>)` `translateY(<translation-value>)` `translateZ(<translation-value>)`	Translation amount in the X/Y/Z direction
`scale(<number> + [, <number>])`	2 parameters of a 2D scaling vector
`scale3d(<number>, <number>, <number>)`	3 parameters of a 3D scaling vector
`scaleX(<number>)`	Scale operation using the X scaling vector, which is given as the parameter
`scaleY(<number>)`	Scale operation using the Y scaling vector, which is given as the parameter
`rotate3d(<number>, <number>, <number>, <angle>)`	Clockwise 3D rotation defined by 3 parameters

CSS Function	Description

`rotateX(<angle>)`
`rotateY(<angle>)`
`rotateZ(<angle>)`
	Clockwise rotation angle along the X/Y/Z-axis

`skewX(<angle>)` `skewY(<angle>)`	Skew transformation angle along the X/Y-axis
`skew(<angle> + [, <angle>])`	Skew transformation angle along both X & Y-axis
`perspective(<length>)`	Perspective projection matrix

Generated Content

Property	Values	
bookmark-label ❸	Model	content | <attr> | <string>
	Description	Initial value: 0. Defines a bookmark label.
	Example	`.class1 {bookmark-label: "review";}`
bookmark-level ❸	Model	none | <integer>
	Description	Defines a bookmark level.
	Example	`.class1 {bookmark-level: 1;}`
bookmark-target ❸	Model	self | <URL> | <attr>
	Description	Defines target of bookmark link
	Example	`.class1 {bookmark-target: url(page.html);}`
border-length ❸	Model	<length> | auto
	Description	Applicable to define the length of a horizontal footnote rule.
	Example	`.class1 {border-length: 50px;}`
float-offset ❸	Model	<length> <length>
	Description	Initial value: 0 0. Defines an offset when floated elements pushed in the opposite direction of the floating.
	Example	`.class1 {outline-offset: 3px;}`

Property	Values	
hyphenate-after ❸	Model	<integer> | <u>auto</u>
hyphenate-before	Description	Defines the minimum number of characters in a word after/ before the hyphenation
	Example	`.class1 {hyphenate-after: 3;}`
hyphenate-character❸	Model	<u>auto</u> | <text_string>
	Description	Defines a shown character when a hyphenation occurs
	Example	`.class1 {hyphenate-character: "\2010";}`
hyphenate-lines ❸	Model	<u>no-limit</u> | <integer>
	Description	Defines the maximum number of hyphenated lines
	Example	`.class1 {hyphenate-lines: 3;}`
hyphenate-resource ❸	Model	<u>none</u> | <URL>
	Description	Initial value: **0**. Defines a comma-separated list of external resources that can assist the browser to determine hyphenation method.
	Example	`.class1 {hyphenate-resource: url("page.html");}`
hyphens ❸	Model	none | <u>manual</u> | auto
	Description	Applies to: inline element. ■ none: no hyphenation ■ manual: words are only hyphenated if there are characters inside the word that suggest line breaks ■ auto: automatic hyphenation determined by characters inside word, or resources listed in the 'hyphenate-resource' property
	Example	`.class1 {hyphens: none;}`
image-resolution ❸	Model	<u>normal</u> | auto | <dpi> [, normal | <dpi>]
	Description	Defines *dot-per-inch* pixel resolution for bitmap images
	Example	`.class1 {image-resolution: 72dpi;}`
marks ❸	Model	[crop + cross] | <u>none</u>
	Description	Crop and cross marks definition which normally used for printing.
	Example	`.class1 {marks: crop  cross;}`

Property	Values	
string-set ❸	Model	[[<identifier> <content-list>] + [,*]]	<u>none</u>
	Description	Defines a comma-separated list of text strings. ■ <string>: e.g. "John" ■ <counter>: counter() or counters() ■ <content>: - 'self': content of the element, excluding the content of its `::before` and `::after` pseudo-element. - 'before': content of the `::before` pseudo-element - 'after': content of the `::after` pseudo-element - 'first-letter': the first letter of the content
	Example	`.class1 {string-set: header "Chapter " counter(header) ": " self;}`
text-replace ❸	Model	[<string> <string>]	<u>none</u>
	Description	Replaces all occurrences of a certain string with another string
	Example	`.class1 {text-replace: "America" "USA";}`

Line Box

This module specifies the properties of line within block elements, baseline alignment and the placement of drop cap initial letters. Most of the properties are new to CSS3.

Property	Values	
alignment-baselinev ❸	Model	<u>baseline</u>	use-script	before-edge	text-before-edge	after-edge	text-after-edge	central	middle	ideographic	alphabetic	hanging	mathematical
	Description	Inline elements. Defines alignment method to the baseline of its parent.
	Example	`.class1 {alignment-baseline: hanging;}`
baseline-shift ❸	Model	<u>baseline</u>	sub	super	<percentage>	<length>
	Description	Inline element. Defines alignment relative to dominant-baseline ■ baseline: no baseline shift ■ sub: subscript ■ super: superscript ■ <length_%>	<length_fixed>: shift based on specific value
	Example	`.class1 {baseline-shift: 5px;}`

Property	Values		
alignment-adjust ❸	Model		auto | baseline | before-edge | text-before-edge | middle | central | after-edge | text-after-edge | ideographic | alphabetic | hanging | mathematical | <length_%> | <length_fixed>
	Description		Inline elements. Defines precise alignment of elements lacking the desired baseline. The element alignment points at the intersection of:
			■ auto: browser defined
			■ baseline: start-edge / dominant-baseline
			■ before-edge: start-edge / before-edge
			■ text-before-edge: start-edge / 'text-before-edge'
			■ central: start-edge / 'central' baseline
			■ middle: start-edge / 'middle' baseline
			■ after-edge: start-edge / after-edge
			■ text-after-edge: start-edge / 'text-after-edge' baseline
			■ ideographic: start-edge / 'ideographic' baseline
			■ alphabetic: start-edge / 'alphabetic' baseline
			■ hanging: start-edge / 'hanging' baseline
			■ mathematical: start-edge / 'mathematical' baseline.
			The alignment point is on the start-edge:
			■ <length_%>: value multiplied by calculated 'line-height'
			■ <length_fixed>: offset lengths of the start-edge
	Example		.class1 {alignment-adjust: text-after-edge;}
dominant-baseline ❸	Model		auto | use-script | no-change | reset-size | alphabetic | hanging | ideographic | mathematical | central | middle | text-after-edge | text-before-edge
	Description		Inline elements. Definition of a scaled-baseline-table value based on three components:
			- baseline-identifier for the dominant baseline
			- script-related definition for additional baseline-identifiers
			- baseline-table font-size
	Example		.class1 {dominant-baseline: ideographic;}
drop-initial-after-adjust	Model		central | middle | after-edge | text-after-edge | ideographic | alphabetic | hanging | mathematical | <percentage> | <length>
	Description		Applies to: ::first-letter pseudo element
			Drop cap alignment for the primary connection point
	Example		.class1 {drop-initial-after-adjust: 2px;}

Property	Values	
drop-initial-after-align ❸	Model	<'alignment-baseline'>
	Description	Applies to: `::first-letter` pseudo element. Defines alignment line within the multiple line box. The line number being defined by the 'drop-initial-value' property.
	Example	`.class1 {drop-initial-after-baseline: central;}`
drop-initial-before-adjust ❸	Model	before-edge | <u>text-before-edge</u> | middle | central | after-edge | text-after-edge | ideographic | hanging | mathematical | <percentage> | <length>
	Description	Applies to: `::first-letter` pseudo element
	Example	`.class1 {drop-initial-before-adjust: hanging;}`
drop-initial-before-align ❸	Model	<u>caps-height</u> | <'alignment-baseline'>
	Description	Applies to: `::first-letter` pseudo element. Defines the alignment line at the secondary connection point
	Example	`.class1 {drop-initial-before-align: before-edge;}`
drop-initial-size ❸	Model	<u>auto</u> | <line> | <length> | <percentage>
	Description	Applies to: `::first-letter` pseudo element Defines the partial dropping of the initial letter. Values other than 'auto' remove the secondary connection line constraint. The drop initial letter is sized using: ■ auto: typographic font attributes ■ <line_number>: number of lines (e.g. integer) ■ <length>: absolute length value (e.g. pixels) ■ <percentage>: relative length value (e.g. %)
	Example	`.class1 {drop-initial-size: 4;}`
drop-initial-value ❸	Model	<u>initial</u> | <integer>
	Description	Applies to: `::first-letter` pseudo element. Defines number of lines occupied by a drop cap letter
	Example	`.class1 {drop-initial-value: 3;}`
inline-box-align ❸	Model	initial | last | <integer>
	Description	Inline-block-level elements. Identifies which line of a multi-line text block aligns with the previous and next element. ■ initial: the initial line ■ last: the last line ■ <integer>: specifies the line number
	Example	`.class1 {inline-box-align: last;}`

Property	Values	
line-height ❸	Model	<u>normal</u> | number | <length> <percentage> | none
	Description	Inherited. All elements. Specifies a standard distance between two text baselines. This value also called 'leading' in traditional typography.
	Example	`.class1 {line-height: 2em;}`
line-stacking ❸	Model	<'line-stacking-strategy'> + <'line-stacking-ruby'> + <'line-stacking-shift'>
	Description	Inherited. Block elements. Shorthand property. Definition for the line box spacing rules.
	Example	`p {line-stacking: include-ruby disregard-shifts;}`
line-stacking-ruby ❸	Model	<u>exclude-ruby</u> | include-ruby
	Description	Inherited. Block elements. Line stacking method for elements containing elements with 'display: ruby-text' or 'display: ruby-text-container'. The ruby annotation elements are: ■ exclude-ruby: ignored for line stacking. ■ include-ruby: considered for line stacking.
	Example	`.class1 {line-stacking-ruby: include-ruby;}`
line-stacking-shift ❸	Model	<u>consider-shifts</u> | disregard-shifts
	Description	Inherited. Block elements. Line stacking method for elements with 'baseline-shift' attribute. The stack-height definition: ■ consider-shifts: considers top-edge and bottom-edge of characters with a 'baseline-shift' property. ■ disregard-shifts: disregards top-edge and bottom-edge of characters with a 'baseline-shift' property.
	Example	`.class1 {line-stacking-shift: disregard-shifts;}`
line-stacking-strategy ❸	Model	<u>inline-line-height</u> | block-line-height | max-height | grid-height
	Description	Inherited. Block elements. Defines the line stacking method. When all inline elements are properly aligned, the stack-height is based on: ■ inline-line-height: the smallest value that contains the **extended** block progression dimension ■ block-line-height: 'line-height' property value ■ max-height: the smallest value that contains the block progression dimension ■ grid-height: smallest multiple of the block element 'line-height' computed value that can contain the block progression
	Example	`.class1 {line-stacking-strategy: grid-height;}`

Property	Values	
text-height ❸	Model	auto	font-size	text-size	max-size
	Description	Inherited. Applies to: inline elements and parents of element with 'display: ruby-text' property. Defines the block-progression dimension of the text content area, which is: ■ auto: based either on the em square determined by the element font-size property value or the cell-height (ascender + descender). ■ font-size: based on the em square as determined by the font size ■ text-size: based on the cell-height (ascender + descender) related to the element font-size. ■ max-size: based on the maximum extent toward the before-edge and after-edge of the box obtained by considering all children elements located on the same line, ruby elements with 'display:ruby-text' property and baseline shifted elements.
	Example	.class1 {text-height: text-size;}
vertical-align ❸	Model	auto	use-script	baseline	sub	super	top	text-top	central	middle	bottom	text-bottom	<percentage>	<length>
	Description	Shorthand property. Applies to: inline-level and 'table-cell' elements. Defines vertical alignment of the **inline** box with the **parent** box via these values:

	inline box	parent box
■ auto	Baseline	Baseline
■ use-script	Computed script baseline	Baseline
■ baseline	Alphabetic baseline	Alphabetic baseline
■ central	Central baseline	Central baseline
■ middle	Middle baseline	Middle baseline
■ sub	Lower baseline	Proper position for subscripts
■ super	Higher baseline	Proper position for superscripts
■ text-top	Top of box	Before-edge of the font
■ text-bottom	Bottom of box	After-edge of the font
■ <percentage> ■ <length>	Alphabetic baseline adjusted by value	Alphabetic baseline
■ top	Before edge of the extended inline box	Before-edge of the line box
■ bottom	After edge of the extended inline box	After-edge of the line box

	Example	.class1 {vertical-align: super;}

Ruby

Ruby is a short caption/annotation text next to the base text, typically used in ideographic East Asian scripts. The CSS Rubi properties associated with the 'Ruby' HTML elements.

Rubi HTML structure	Rubi CSS Box Model

`<ruby>`
蘋果`<rt>apple</rt>`
`</ruby>`
	`<rt>apple</rt>` ← Rubi Text
	蘋果 ← Rubi Base ← Rubi Group
	
	apple
	蘋果

Property	Values		
'ruby-align' ❸	Model		auto	start	left	center	end	right	distribute-letter	distribute-space	line-edge

	Description		Inherited. Applies to: all elements & generated content. Defines the text alignment of the ruby text and ruby base contents relative to each other:
			■ auto: browser defined value. It is generally equal to the 'centered' value
			■ start
				left: the start edge of the base
				■ center: centered within the width of the base
				■ end
					right: end edge of the base.
					■ distribute-letter: the ruby text content is evenly distributed across the width of the base. No white space is added preceding the first and following the last character in the ruby text.
					■ distribute-space: the ruby text content is evenly distributed across the width of the base. White space is added preceding the first and following the last character in the ruby text.
					■ line-edge:
					  - If the ruby text is not adjacent to a side edge, the 'auto' value applies
					  - If the ruby text is adjacent to a side edge, the 'auto' value applies, and the side of the ruby text is lined up with the corresponding edge of the base

	Example		`.class1 {ruby-align: distribute-letter;}`
'ruby-position' ❸	Model		before	after	right	inline
	Description		Applies to: the parent of elements with `display:ruby-text` property. Defines the position of the ruby text relative to its base.
	Example		`.class1 {ruby-position: after;}`

Property	Values	
'ruby-overhang' ❸	Model	auto | start | end | <u>none</u>
	Description	Inherited. Applies to: parent of elements with **display:ruby-text** property. Defines ruby text overhang methods over any adjacent text when the ruby text is wider than the its base: ■ auto: text overhang is allowed on either side of the base ■ start: preceding text overhang is allowed ■ end: text overhang is allowed at the end of the base ■ none: text overhang is not allowed on either side of the base
	Example	`.class1 {ruby-overhang: end;}`
'ruby-span' ❸	Model	attr(x) | <u>none</u>
	Description	Applies to: elements with **display:ruby-text** property. Defines two methods *Rubi* elements span: ■ attr(x): The value of attribute '**x**' as a string value evaluated as a <number>, the computed value, to determine the number of ruby base elements to be spanned by the annotation element. ■ none: no span, the computed value is '**1**'.
	Example	`.class1 {ruby-span: attr(rbspan);}`

Hyperlink Presentation

Property	Values	
target	Model	<target-name> + <target-new> + <target-position>
	Description	New in *CSS3*. Applies to: hyperlinks. Shorthand property. Hyperlink target definition. The browser support is inconsistent.
	Example	`.class1 {target: "Feedback" tab front;}`
target-name ❸	Model	<u>current</u> | root | parent | new | modal | <string>
	Description	Applies to: hyperlinks. Defines the target values: ■ current: the link current frame, tab or window where ■ root: the current tab or window ■ parent: the parent of the current frame. If the current frame has no parent, this value is treated as 'root'. ■ new: a new destination is always created. This property is a dependency for the 'target-new' property. ■ modal: a new temporary modal window ■ <string>: specifies a name for the existing frame, window or tab. If the named destination does not exists, a new destination is created with that name.
	Example	`.class1 {target-name: "Feedback";}`

Property	Values	
target-new ❸	Model	window	tab	none
	Description	Applies to: hyperlinks. Specifies a standard distance between two text baselines. This value also called 'leading' in traditional typography.
	Example	.class1 {target-new: tab;}
target-position ❸	Model	above	behind	front	back
	Description	Applies to: hyperlinks. Defines a method of overlap for the new hyperlink destination
	Example	.class1 {target-position: front;}

Paged Media

CSS3 paged media is defined alternatively to a continuous media describing page specific behavior and elements:

- Page breaks
- Page size, orientation, margins, border, and padding
- Headers, footers and page numbering
- Widows and orphans
- In the page model, the document appears in a CSS 'page box'. It consists of border , margin, padding and other properties. The properties of a page box are determined by the *@page* rule set
- Page box size specified by the 'size' property.

Property	Values	
fit ❸	Model	fill	hidden	meet	slice
	Description	Applies to: replaced elements, typically images. Defines the scale method if neither 'width' nor 'height' property is 'auto':
		▪ fill: scale the object's height and width independently so that the content fills the containing box
		▪ hidden: no scale
		▪ meet: scale as large as possible while preserving the aspect ratio
		- width <= 'width' and height <= 'height'
		- fit at least one smaller side (vertical or horizontal)
		▪ slice: scale the object as small as possible while preserving the aspect ratio
		- its width >= 'width' and height >= 'height'
		- fit at least one larger side
	Example	.class1 {fit: meet;}

Property	Values	
fit-position ❸	Model	[[<percentage> | <length>]{1,2} | [[top | center | bottom] + [left | center | right]]] | auto
	Description	Initial value: **0% 0%**. Inherited. Applies to: replaced elements, typically images. Defines the object alignment inside the box. The values are similar to the 'background-position' values.
	Example	`.class1 {fit-position: 10% left;}`
image-orientation ❸	Model	<u>auto</u> | <angle>
	Description	Applies to: images. Defines the image angle.
	Example	`.class1 {image-orientation: 90deg;}`
orphans	Model	<integer>
widows	Description	Initial value: **2**. Inherited. Applies to: block-level elements.
		Defines a minimum number of lines of a paragraph that must be left at the bottom (orphans) or top (widows) of a page.
	Example	`.class1 {orphans: 3; widows: 3;}`
page	Model	<u>auto</u> | <identifier>
	Description	Inherited. Applies to: block-level elements.
		Specifies the page type where an element should be displayed. If a block box with inline content has a 'page' property that is different from the preceding block box, then page break(s) would be inserted between them. The boxes after the page break are rendered on a page box of the named type.

	Example 1	`/* tables are rendered on a right-hand side portrait page titled 'rotated' */`
		
		`@page vericale {size: portrait;}`
		
		`table {page: vericale; page-break-before: right}`

	Example 2	`/* CSS: tables are rendered on portrait pages while the page type 'wide' is valid for the the rest of the <div> content */`
		`@page wide {size: 20cm 10cm;}`
		`@page vericale {size: portrait;}`
		
		`div {page: wide;}`
		`table {page: vericale;}`
		
		`// the HTML document:`
		`<div>`
		
		`<table><tr><td></td></tr></table>`
		`<table><tr><td></td></tr></table>`
		
		`<p>This is rendered on a 'wide' page</p></div>`

Property	Values	
page-break-after	Model	<u>auto</u> | always | avoid | left | right
page-break-before	Description	Applies to: block-level elements. Defines page break method before (after) the generated box: ■ auto: no forced / avoided page break ■ always: forced page break ■ avoid: avoided page break ■ left | right: forced page break; the next page is formatted as a left / right page
	Example	`.class1 {page-break-after: always;}`
page-break-inside	Model	<u>auto</u> | avoid
	Description	Applies to: block-level elements. Defines a printing page break within an element. An 'avoid ' value attempts to avoid a page break within the element.
	Example	`.class1 {page-break-inside: avoid;}`
size	Model	\<length\>{1,2} | <u>auto</u> | [\<page-size\> + [portrait | landscape]]

	Description	Applies to: page context. Defines the size and orientation of the containing box for page content.
		
		The size of a page box may either be "absolute" (fixed size) or "relative" (scalable, fluid). Relative pages automatically scale the document and make optimal use of the page size. The relative values:
		■ auto: size and orientation of the page is set by the browser.
		■ landscape | portrait: horizontal / vertical orientation
		The absolute values:
		■ \<length\>: length can be set in fixed units (e.g. inches)
		■ \<page-size\>: 'Media Standardized Names' based width x height:
		  - A5: 148mm x 210 mm
		  - A4: 210 mm x 297 mm
		  - A3: 297mm x 420mm
		  - B5: 176mm x 250mm
		  - B4: 250mm wide by 353mm
		  - letter: North American letter, 8.5 inches x 11 inches
		  - legal: North American legal, 8.5 inches x 14 inches
		  - ledger: North American tabloid, 11 inches x 17 inches

	Example	`@page {size: B5 landscape;}`

User Interface (UI)

Property	Values	
appearance ❸	Model	normal	<appearance>
	Description	Applies to: all elements. Shorthand for 'appearance', 'color', 'font', and 'cursor'. Defines an element as a standard platform UI element. The term "platform" generally has a meaning of a native operating system (or browser) graphical rendering engine. ■ The property sets 'appearance' to the specified value and the other properties to their appropriate system value, rendering element using platform-specific user interface control. ■ normal: resets 'appearance' to 'normal' and the others to 'inherit'

	Example	`input[type=button] {appearance: push-button;}`
		`<!--default browser look and feel:-->`
		`input[type=button].custom {color: blue; background-color: yellow;}`
		
		`<!--the related HTML5 code:-->`
		`<input type=button value="plain button">`
		`<input type=button value="color button" class=custom>`

box-sizing ❸	Model	content-box	border-box
	Description	Applies to: elements accepting width or height. ■ content-box: the specified width and height (and respective min/max properties) apply to the content box of the element ■ border-box: the specified width and height on this element define the border box of the element. The content size is calculated by subtracting the border and padding values.

	Example	`div.hSplit {`
		`box-sizing: border-box; width: 50%; float: left;}`
		
		`<!--the related HTML5 code:-->`
		`  <div style=width:200px>`
		
		`  <div class=hSplit>The left half.</div>`
		`  <div class=hSplit>The right half.</div>`
		
		`</div>`

content	Model	icon
	Description	The CSS 2.1 pseudo-element is replaced by the 'icon' property, and treated as a replaced element
	Example	`img {content: icon;}`

Property	Values	
cursor ❸	Model	[[<URL> [<x> <y>]]* [auto	default	none	context-menu	help	pointer	progress	wait	cell	crosshair	text	vertical-text	alias	copy	move	no-drop	not-allowed	e-resize	n-resize	ne-resize	nw-resize	s-resize	se-resize	sw-resize	w-resize	ew-resize	ns-resize	nesw-resize	nwse-resize	col-resize	row-resize	all-scroll]]
	Description	Inherited. Applies to: all elements.

Image cursors:

- <URL>: cursor image referenced by URL.
- <x> <y>: The optional <x> and <y> coordinates define the position within the image or hotspot

General purpose cursors

- auto: context-based cursor determined by browser
- default: platform-dependent default cursor, typically an arrow
- none

Links and status cursors

- context-menu: object context menu, e.g. arrow with a menu-like graphic
- help: reference to a help, e.g. question mark or a balloon
- pointer: a link indicator
- progress: program processing indicator, but user still can interact with the program, e.g. spinning ball, watch or hourglass
- wait: watch or hourglass

Selection cursors

- cell: cell selection cursor, e.g. a thick plus sign with a dot in the middle
- crosshair: a "+" sign cursor. Indicates a 2D bitmap selection mode
- text: text selection indicator, e.g. a vertical I-beam
- vertical-text: vertical text selection indicator, e.g. a horizontal I-beam

Drag and drop cursors

- alias: alias/shortcut indicator, e.g. an arrow cursor
- copy: object is being copied indicator, e.g. arrow with a plus sign
- move: object is being moved indicator
- no-drop: Indicates that the dragged item cannot be dropped, e.g. a hand or pointer with a small circle with a line through it
- not-allowed: action not allowed indicator, e.g. circle with a line through it

Resizing and scrolling cursors

- e-resize, n-resize, ne-resize, nw-resize, s-resize, se-resize, sw-resize, w-resize: an edge is to be moved indicator
- ew-resize, ns-resize, nesw-resize, nwse-resize: bidirectional resize indicator
- col-resize: column resize indicator, e.g. arrows pointing left and right
- row-resize: column resize indicator, e.g. arrows pointing up and down
- all-scroll: any direction scroll indicator, e.g. 4 directional arrows

	Example	:link,:visited { cursor: crosshair;}

Property	Values	
icon ❸	Model	auto	[<URL> + [,*]]
	Description	Applies to: all elements. An element could be styled with an iconic equivalent
		■ auto: generic default browser icon
		■ <URL>: the icon values referenced by <URL> in a comma delimited list. This permits the usage of multiple icon formats for various platforms and media types

	Example	`img, object {content:icon;}`
		`img {icon:url(image1.jpg);}`
		`object {icon:url(image2.gif);}`

nav-index ❸	Model	auto	<number>
	Description	Applies to: all enabled elements. Tabbing order definition.
	Example	`.class1 {nav-index: 2;}`
nav-up ❸ nav-right nav-down nav-left	Model	auto	<id> [current	root	<target-name>]
	Description	Applies to: all elements.
		■ auto: browser defined.
		■ <id>: consists of a '#' character followed by a unique ID.
		■ <target-name>: text string, a target frame for the navigation. The keyword 'root' indicates the full window.
	Example	`.class1 {nav-up: #a1 root;}`
outline	Model	<'outline-color'> + <'outline-style'> + <'outline-width'>
	Description	Applies to: all elements. Shorthand property.
		The outline is always on top, drawn "over" a box, and it doesn't influence the position or size of the box. Outlines could be non-rectangular. The outline has the same property values on all sides, e.g., there are no 'outline-top' or 'outline-right' properties.
	Example	`.class1 {outline: blue thick solid;}`
outline-color	Model	<color>	invert
	Description	Applies to: all elements.
	Example	`.class1 {outline-color: #fff;}`
outline-offset	Model	<length>
	Description	Applies to: all elements.
	Example	`.class1 {outline-offset: 5px;}`

Property	Values	
outline-style	Model	auto | <border-style>
	Description	Initial value: none. Applies to: all elements.
		The 'outline-style' property accepts the same values as 'border-style' property plus the value 'auto', minus 'hidden'.
	Example	.class1 {outline-style: auto;}
outline-width	Model	<border-width>
	Description	Initial value: **medium**. Applies to: all elements. The values are the same values as the 'border-width' property values.
	Example	.class1 {outline-width: thin;}
resize ❸	Model	none | both | horizontal | vertical
	Description	Applies to: elements with 'overflow' value other than visible.
		Defines the user-resize capability and axis/axes.
	Example	.class1 {resize: horizontal;}

Pseudo-Classes

Pseudo-Class	Values	
:active	Description	Activated element
	Example	a:active {color: blue;}
:focus	Description	Element has focus
	Example	a:focus {color: black;}
:hover	Description	Element has mouse over
	Example	a:hover {text-decoration: underline;} a:focus:hover {color: red;}
:visited :link	Description	Mutually exclusive pseudo-classes represent visited / unvisited link. ■ The 1st example defines the font color of all visited links. ■ The 2nd example defines the font color of all unvisited HTML links with a class 'resources'.
	Example	a:visited {color: blue;} a.resources:link {color: black;}
:enabled ❸ :disabled	Description	Mutually exclusive pseudo-classes represent enabled / disabled element
	Example	a:enabled {color: blue;} a:disabled {color: black;}

Pseudo-Class	Values	
:checked ❸	Description	Element checked state (e.g., a check box)
	Example	`a:checked {color: blue;}`
:lang(code)	Model	:lang(<language code>) { }
	Description	Element language definition
	Example	`:lang(fr) {color: blue;}`
:nth-child(n) ❸	Model	:nth-child({ <number expression> | odd | even }) { }
	Description	Matches any element that is the **n**-th child of its parent. **:nth-child(an+b)** element that has **an+b-1** siblings before it, for any positive integer or zero value of **n**, and has a parent element. For values of **a** and **b** > 0, this divides the element's children into groups of **a** elements (the last group taking the remainder), and selecting the **b**-th element of each group. This allows to alternate the color of every other row in a table. The 1st child index is **1**.
	Example 1	Selecting a third child: `:nth-child(3) {color: blue;}`

	Example 2a	Two ways of selecting every odd row of a table :
		`tr:nth-child(2n+1)  {color: navy;}`
		`:nth-child(odd)     {color: green;}`

	Example 2b	Three ways of selecting every even row of a table:
		`tr:nth-child(2n+0)`
		`tr:nth-child(2n)`
		`tr:nth-child(even)`

	Example 3	Alternate paragraph colors in sets of 3:
		`p:nth-child(3n+1)`
		`p:nth-child(3n+2)`
		`p:nth-child(3n+3)`

	Example 4	When the value **b** is preceded by a "-", the "+" character is effectively replaced by the "-" character indicating the negative value of **b**. Example of electing the 9th, 19th, 29th, etc elements:
		`:nth-child(10n-1)`
		`:nth-child(10n+9)`

:nth-last-child(n) ❸	Model	:nth-last-child({ <number expression> | odd | even }) { }
	Description	The **n**-th sibling counting from the last sibling.
	Example 1	The two last rows of a table: `tr:nth-last-child(-n+2)`
	Example 2	Selecting the last 5 list items in a list: `li:nth-last-child(-n+5)`

Pseudo-Class	Values	
:nth-of-type(n) ❸	Model	:nth-of-type({ <number expression> | odd | even }) { }
	Description	The **n**-th sibling of its type.
	Example	Selecting the 2nd, 5th, 8th, etc, paragraphs in a **div** element: `div > p:nth-of-type(3n-1)`
:nth-last-of-type(n) ❸	Model	:nth-last-of-type({ <number expression> | odd | even }) { }
	Description	The **n**-th sibling of its type counting from the last sibling

	Example	Two ways of selecting all h3 children except the first and last:
		`body > h3:nth-of-type(n+2):nth-last-of-type(n+2) { }`
		`body > h3:not(:first-of-type):not(:last-of-type) { }`

:first-child ❸ :last-child :only-child	Description	The first sibling, the last sibling, the only child element
	Example	`li:first-child {color: blue;}`
:last-of-type ❸ :first-of-type :only-of-type	Description	The 1st sibling of its type, the last sibling & the only child of that type
	Example	`li:first-of-type {color: blue;}`
:empty ❸	Description	Element has no children
:root ❸	Description	Document root *HTML* element
:target ❸	Description	URL-defined target element. Target is specified by a number sign (#) followed by an anchor ID, called the fragment identifier. URLs with fragment identifier link to an element within the document, known as the target element. By applying the **:target** pseudo class selector, CSS can only style the elements on the page that match the anchor chosen. For example, this URL pointing to an anchor 'products': **http://example.com/top.html#products**. A target **DIV** element can be styled by the **:target** pseudo-class.

	Example	`<style>div:target {color:blue;}</style>`
		
		`<a href=#products>Products/a>`
		
		`<div id=products>Product description</div>`

:indeterminate ❸	Description	Radio and checkbox elements can be toggled, but are sometimes in an indeterminate state, neither checked nor unchecked.

Pseudo-Class	Values	
:not(x) ❸	Model	:not(simple selector) { }
	Description	This negation pseudo-class would match all elements that do not match an argument in the parenthesis

	Example	`:not(div)  { }`
		`:not('logo')  { }`
		`input:not([type="checkbox"]  { }`

Pseudo-Elements

`::first-letter`	Defines style for the first letter of a paragraph (the drop cap letter)
`::first-line`	Defines style for the first line of a text
`::before`	Inserts content before an element
`::after`	Inserts content after an element
`::selection`	Part of a document that has been highlighted by the user, e.g. text

CSS At-Rules

At-rules are special set of instructions to the CSS interpreter. At-rules are named because of the @ character prefix. @rules can be defined for a specific type of elements or media.

Pseudo-Class	Values	
@character	Description	Character set encoding defined at the top of for the external CSS document
	Example	@charset "iso-8859-1";
@import	Description	Allows nested style sheets by importing one style sheet into another. ■ **@import** declaration must appear before any rules. ■ It could be used to hide certain styles from older browsers, which don't recognize **@import**.
	Example	@import url(mystylesheet.css);
@media	Description	Medi-specific CSS. Some options are: ■ all: every media ■ aural: speech synthesizers ■ braille: braille writing system ■ handheld: for handheld devices ■ print: for printers ■ screen: for computer monitors
	Example	@media print {body {color:blue;}}
@page	Description	Defines border, margin, padding and other properties for paged media
	Example	@page first {size: landscape;}
@font-face	Description	Defines embedding method for custom fonts

	Example	@font-face {
		font-family: VremyaCyrillic;
		src: url(fonts/VremyaCyrillic.ttf) format("opentype");
		unicode-range: U+00-FF, U+980-9FF;}

@namespace	Description	Declares an *XML namespace* and, optionally, a prefix with which we can refer to it. **@namespace** rules must follow all **@charset** and **@import** rules, and precede all other at-rules in a style sheet.
	Example	@namespace "http://www.w3.org/1999/xhtml";

CSS3 Browser Compatibility

	Desktop					Mobile		
	IE	FireFox	Safari	Chrome	Opera	iOS	Opera	Android
Word Wrap	6	3.5	4	6	10.5	3.2	10	2.1
Position: fixed	7	3	3.2	6	10.5	✕	10	2.2*
Opacity	9	3	3.2	6	10.5	3.2	10	2.1
Web Fonts	9	3.5	3.2	6	10.5	4.2	10	2.1*
Table Display	8	3	3.2	6	10.5	3.2	10	2.1
Generated Content	8	3	3.2	6	10.5	3.2	10	2.1
Box Sizing	8	3	3.2	6	10.5	3.2	10	2.1
HSL-Alpha Colors	9	3	3.2	6	10.5	3.2	10	2.1
Border Radius	9	3	3.2	6	10.5	3.2	✕	2.1*
Text Overflow	6*	4?	3.2*	6*	10.5*	3.2*	10*	2.1*
Multi-column Layout	9?	3	3.2	6	11.1	3.2	✕	2.1
Flexible Box Layout	9?	4	3.2	6	11.1?	3.2	✕	2.1
Media Queries	9	3.5	4	6	10.5	3.2	10	2.1
Advanced Selectors	9	3.5	3.2	6	10.5	3.2	10	2.1
Box-Shadow	9	3.5	3.2	6	10.5	3.2	✕	2.1
Transformations	9	3.5	3.2	6	10.5	3.2	✕	2.1
Text Shadow	9?	3.5	4	6	10.5	3.2	10	2.1
Border Images	9?	3.5	3.2	6	10.5	3.2	✕	2.1
Multi-Backgrounds	9	3.6	3.2	6	10.5	3.2	10	2.1
Advanced bg-image	9	4	5	6	10.5	3.2	10	2.1*
SVG/CSS backgrounds	9	4	5	6	10.5	3.2*	10	✕
CSS3 Animation	9?	4?	5	6	11.1?	3.2*	10	✕
CSS3 Transitions	9?	4	3.2	6	10.5	3.2	10	2.1
3D Transforms	9?	4?	5	10?	11.1?	3.2	✕	✕
calc() as unit value	9	4	6?	10?	11.1?	✕	✕	✕
Overall compliance	**72%**	**86%**	**92%**	**88%**	**84%**	**86%**	**64%**	**81%**

* indicates partial support

? indicates unknown support

✕ indicates no support

6. HTML5 APIs

In addition to a new markup specifications, HTML5 offers scripting application programming interfaces (APIs). The HTML5 APIs provide various native Rich Internet Application functionality without the use of plugins, simplifying development and improving user experience.

This chapter provides basic fundamental information about HTML5 APIs which will be expanded in the next addition of this book.

Canvas vs. SVG

HTML5 Canvas and Scalable Vector Graphics (SVG) are fundamentally different Web technologies that allow you to create graphics to be displayed on HTML document.
In the next section we explore those differences and advantages.

Differences and advantages

	Canvas	SVG
Part of HTML5 specification	✓	
W3C recommendation, open standard	✓	✓
XML-based technology, SVG files are pure XML		✓
Image Type: 2D vector imaging with some raster capability		✓
Image Type: 2D raster (bitmap, pixel-based) or 3D WebGL imaging	✓	
High performance 2D image rendering	✓	
Sharp text and data charts rendering		✓
Resolution independent, can scale image and text without degradation of rendering quality (similar to Flash)		✓
Interactivity capabilities: each element is a DOM node and it can be controlled using mouse events and JavaScript, making it a better solution for Web application user interfaces.		✓
Good support for animation using declarative syntax API, or via JavaScript		✓
Better suitable for UI: based on XML with accessibility support		✓
Text is selectable and searchable		✓

Canvas

About Canvas

The HTML5 canvas element uses JavaScript to create web graphics

- A canvas technology is part of HTML5 specification.
- Canvas element creates 2D raster (bitmap) images. Key points about raster Images:
  - composed of square pixels in a grid of columns and rows
  - resolution dependent
  - resizing canvas image degrades quality
  - easily converted to various raster formats
  - restricted to rectangle areas
- The `<canvas>` element has two main attributes - width and height.
- The canvas element has several methods for drawing paths, boxes, circles, characters, and adding images.
- Canvas element can utilize a couple of different options:
  - 2D drawing context,
  - 3D drawing context (WebGL)

Basic HTML document with Canvas element

Description	Code

Head and body	`<!DOCTYPE HTML>`
	`<html><head><title></title></head>`
	`<body>`

Canvas Element with ID
- Includes HTML properties
- Initially empty
- Fallback content
	`<canvas id=canvasImg width=200 height=100 style="border:1px solid gray;">`
	`   This browser does not support the canvas element`
	`</canvas>`

JavaScript Drawing
- Finds Canvas element by ID
- Creates 2D object
	`<script type=text/javascript>`
	`   var c=document.getElementById("canvasImg");`
	`   var cxt=c.getContext("2d");`

- Creates rectangular object: position 10, 10; size 180 x 60	`   cxt.fillRect(10,10,180,60);` `</script>`
	`<body>`

Moving canvas script into a function

Description	Code

Head	```html
	<!DOCTYPE HTML>
	<html><head><title></title>
	
	<script type=text/javascript>
	``

▪ JavaScript function
▪ Creates drawing
 - basic circle
 - position and size attributes
	``javascript
	function drawCircle() {
	  var c=document.getElementById("canvasImg");
	  var cxt=c.getContext("2d");
	
	  cxt.beginPath();
	  cxt.arc(100,100,50,0,Math.PI*2,true);
	  cxt.closePath();
	  cxt.stroke();}
	
	</script> </head>
	``

Body
 	
▪ onLoad event calls function
▪ Canvas Element renders the function-defined drawing
	``html
	<body onload="drawCircle()">
	<canvas id=canvasImg width=200 height=100 style="border:1px solid gray;">
	This browser does not support the canvas element
	</canvas> <body>
	``

Basic Canvas methods and properties

Method or Property	Description
`beginPath()`	Resetting the current path
`moveTo(x, y)`	Creating a new subpath with the point defined
`closePath()`	The current subpath is closed, and a new subpath is started
`fill()`	The subpaths fill and stroke applied using current fill style
`stroke()`	
`fillStyle`	Shape's fill and stroke style
`strokeStyle`	
`bezierCurveTo(cp1x, cp1y, cp2x, cp2y, x, y)`	The point is added to the path, connecting to the previous point by a Bezier curve using control points. The **x** & **y**: the end point coordinates. The **cp1x** & **cp1y** / **cp2x** & **cp2y**: the 1st / 2nd control point coordinates
`quadraticCurveTo(cpx,cpy,x,y)`	The point is added to the current path, connected to the previous point by a quadratic Bezier curve

139

Method or Property	Description
addColorStop(offset, color)	Color stop with a color to the gradient with offset value range of **0.0-1.0**
drawImage(image, dx, dy)	Reference to an image or canvas object with **x** and **y** coordinates
createRadialGradient(x0, y0, r0, x1, y1, r1)	Radial gradient defining a circle with coordinates **(x1,y1)** and radius **r1** and the second a circle with coordinates **(x2,y2)** and radius **r2**
createLinearGradient(x0, y0, x1, y1)	Linear gradient represented by the start **(x1,y1)** & end points **(x2,y2)**
font [= value]	Font settings property
textAlign [= value]	Text alignment property. The values are: start, end, left, right, and center.
textBaseline [= value]	Baseline alignment property. Values are: top, hanging, middle , alphabetic, ideographic and bottom
fillText(text,x,y[, maxWidth])	Text fill property at the coordinates **x** and **y**
strokeText(text, x, y [, maxWidth])	Text stroke property at the coordinates **x** and **y**
createPattern(image, repetition)	Image defined as pattern. The second argument values are: repeat, repeat-x, repeat-y, and no-repeat.
shadowColor [= value]	Shadow color property
shadowOffsetX [= value] shadowOffsetY [= value]	Shadow offset **X** and offset **Y** properties
shadowBlur [= value]	Shadows blur property
save() restore()	Canvas - save and restore states methods
rotate(angle)	Rotate method
scale(x, y)	Scale method: **x** and **y** are horizontal and vertical scale factor parameters
transform(m11, m12, m21, m22, dx, dy)	Transformation matrix defines the matrix given by the arguments
setTransform(m11, m12, m21, m22, dx, dy)	Transformation matrix redefined to the matrix given by the arguments
setInterval(callback, time);	Repeatedly executable code. Time parameter given in milliseconds
setTimeout(callback, time);	Once executable code. Time parameter given in milliseconds

Canvas methods in action: drawing

Object	Code
| Lines | ```
cxt.moveTo(100,160); cxt.lineTo(460,40);
cxt.strokeStyle="blue"; //line color
cxt.lineWidth=4;        //line width
cxt.stroke();
``` |
| Rectangle | ```
cxt.fillRect(15,15,120,60);

cxt.clearRect(20,20,110,50);

cxt.strokeRect(15,15,120,60);
``` |
| Path: circle | ```
cxt.fillStyle="#FF0000";

cxt.beginPath();
cxt.arc(100,100,50,0,Math.PI*2,true);
cxt.closePath();
cxt.stroke();

cxt.fill();
``` |
| Path: triangle | ```
cxt.beginPath();

cxt.moveTo(160,160);
cxt.lineTo(120,50);
cxt.lineTo(50,120);

cxt.closePath();
cxt.stroke();
``` |
| Gradient | ```
var grd=cxt.createLinearGradient(0,0,180,60); //gradient
grd.addColorStop(0, "red"); //red & blue gradient color definition
grd.addColorStop(0.5,"blue");
cxt.fillStyle=grd; //object fill style defined
cxt.fillRect(10,10,100,60); //Creates rectangle
``` |
```

Object	Code
| Oval | ```javascript
var centerX = 200; //oval location and size
var centerY = 50;
var height = 80;
var width = 250;
cxt.beginPath();
cxt.moveTo(centerX,centerY - height/2);

//right half of oval
cxt.bezierCurveTo(centerX+width/2,centerY+height/2,centerX
+width/2,centerY-height/2,centerX,centerY-height/2);

cxt.bezierCurveTo(centerX-width/2, //left half of oval
centerY-height/2,centerX-width/2,
centerY+height/2,centerX, centerY+height/2);

cxt.lineWidth=4;  //fill and stroke styling
cxt.strokeStyle="black"; cxt.stroke();
cxt.fillStyle="#C9A761"; cxt.fill();
cxt.closePath();
``` |
| Raster Image | ```javascript
var img = new Image();

img.src = '/images/portrait.jpg';
``` |

Scalable Vector Graphic (SVG)

SVG is an XML-based language for 2-D vector graphics.

- SVG is not part of HTML5 specification, however it is an W3C open standard
- Images created using geometrical element such as points, lines, Bézier curves, and shapes, which are based on mathematical equations
- SVG images can be scaled without degradation, behaving similarly to Flash graphics
- SVG files are pure XML files which could be created in any text editor
- Currently Adobe Illustrator and some other tools are capable of exporting and importing SVG graphics. Eventually we should expect more visual SVG authoring tools
- SVG can be created
  - inline: within the HTML document
  - by embedding a stand alone .SVG file

Basic HTML document with inline SVG

Description	Code
Head and body	```<!DOCTYPE HTML>``` ```<html><head><title></title></head><body>```
Defines an SVG document fragment	```<svg xmlns=http://www.w3.org/2000/svg>```

■ Defines a rectangle with fill, stroke, position and size attributes
 	
■ Fallback content
	```<rect stroke=black fill=blue stroke-width=2 x=15px y=15px width=200px height=100px>```
	
	```This browser does not support the canvas element```
	
	```</svg>```
	```<body>```

Ways of creating SVG in HTML Document

Technique	Commentary	
<embed> tag	Description	The **<embed>** tag is not a standard HTML tag. It utilizes Adobe SVG Viewer. The **<embed>** tag is not compatible with a valid XHTML document
	Example	```<embed src=image.svg width=200 height=200 type=image/svg+xml pluginspage=http://www.adobe.com/svg/viewer/install/>```
<object> tag	Description	The **<object>** tag is a standard HTML tag and is supported by all modern browsers. This method does not allow scripting.
	Example	```<object data=image.svg width=200 height=200 type=image/svg+xml codebase=http://www.adobe.com/svg/viewer/install/>```
<iframe> tag	Description	The **<iframe>** tag can be used to render SVG graphics.
	Example	```<iframe src="image.svg" width="90" height="90"></iframe>```
Inline	Description	Inline SVG only with XHTML5 document, using MIME Type **application/xhtml+xml** or **text/xml**, or in modern browsers

	Example	```<svg width="200" height="200" version="1.1" xmlns="http://www.w3.org/2000/svg">```
		
		```<circle cx="100" cy="80" r="60" stroke="#ffffff" stroke-width="1" fill="blue">```
		
		```</svg>```

Technique	Commentary	
JavaScript	Description	JavaScript can be used to create canvas, graphic object (circle) and object attributes

	Example	```<div id="svgimage"></div>```
		
		```<script type="text/javascript">```
		
		```var svg = document.createElementNS ("http://www.w3.org/2000/svg", "svg"), circle = document.createElementNS ("http://www.w3.org/2000/svg", "circle");```
		
		```svg.setAttribute("version", "1.1"); circle.setAttribute("r", "60"); circle.setAttribute("cx", "100"); circle.setAttribute("cy", "80"); circle.setAttribute("fill", "blue"); circle.setAttribute("stroke", "black"); svg.appendChild(circle); document.getElementById("svgimage").appendChild(svg);```
		
		```</script>```

Raphaël JavaScript Library	Description	Raphaël is a small JavaScript library that could be used to build vector graphics. The **raphael.js** file can be downloaded and included into the **<head>** of HTML document. Various predefined shapes and transformations then can be accessed from the library.

raphaeljs.com	Example	```var paper = Raphael(10, 50, 320, 200);```
		
		```// Creates circle at x = 50, y = 40, with radius 10 var circle = paper.circle(50, 40, 10);```
		
		```// Sets the fill and stroke attributes circle.attr("fill", "blue"); circle.attr("stroke", "black");```

SVG Shapes

Object	Code	Description

	```<?xml version="1.0" standalone="no"?>```
	```<!DOCTYPE svg PUBLIC "-//W3C//DTD SVG 1.1//```
	```EN" "http://www.w3.org/Graphics/SVG/1.1/DTD/```
	```svg11.dtd">```
	
	```<svg width="100%" height="100%" version="1.1"```
	```xmlns="http://www.w3.org/2000/svg">```
	
	```<rect width="300" height="100"/>```
	
	```</svg>```
		Sample stand-alone, self-contained SVG document. The code can be created in text editor and saved, e.g. image.svg

Circle	```<circle cx="100" cy="80" r="60"``` ```stroke="black" stroke-width="1" fill="blue"/>```	Common properties ■ r: radius

Ellipse	```<ellipse cx="300" cy="150" rx="200" ry="80"```
	```style="fill:green;"```
	```stroke:rgb(0,0,100); stroke-width:2"/>```
		■ x & y: left and right position
		■ cx: x of the center coordinate
		■ cy: y of the center coordinate

Line	```<line x1="0" y1="0" x2="300" y2="300"``` ```style="stroke:black; stroke-width:2"/>```	■ rx: horizontal radius ■ ry: vertical radius

Polygon	```<polygon points="200,100 350,220 150,260"```
	```style="fill:blue; stroke:#000;```
	```stroke-width:1"/>```
		Path data commands
		
		■ A: elliptical Arc

Polyline	```<polyline points="0,0 0,20 20,20 20,30 30,```
	```40 40,60" style="fill:white; stroke:red;```
	```stroke-width:2"/>```
		■ C: 'curveto'
		■ H: horizontal 'lineto'
		■ L: 'lineto'
		■ M: 'moveto'

Rectangle	```<rect x="30" y="30" rx="30" ry="30"```
	```width="240" height="120"```
	```style="fill:red; stroke:black;```
	```stroke-width:3; opacity:0.7"/>```
		■ S: smooth 'curveto'
		■ Q: quadratic Belzier curve
		■ T: smooth quadratic Belzier curve
		■ V: vertical 'lineto'

Path	```<path d="M250 150 L150 350 L350 350 Z"/>```	■ Z: closepath

Audio and Video

Embedding audio and video

HTML5 provides simple native, plugin-free, audio and video support without the need for Flash. HTML5 provides rich scripting API for playback control. Adding video/audio to a web page is almost as simple as adding an image.

The API also defines events that can control media playback and load state.

Description	Code

Basic method of embedding video	```html
	<body>
	<video src=myVideo.mp4 width=320 height=240 controls>
	Your browser does not support the <video> element
	</video>
	</body>
	``

Basic method of embedding audio	```html
	<audio src=myAudio.wav controls autoplay>
	Your browser does not support the <audio> element
	</audio>
	``

A video and audio elements allow multiple source elements. The **<source>** tag could be used to assign attributes	```html
	<video width=320 height=240 controls autoplay>
	    <source src=/videos/movie1.ogg type=video/ogg/>
	    <source src=/videos/movie2.mp4 type=video/mp4/>
	Your browser does not support the <video> element
	</video>
	<audio controls autoplay>
	    <source src=/audio/audio.ogg type=audio/ogg/>
	    <source src=/audio/audio.wav type=audio/wav/>
	Your browser does not support the <audio> element
	</audio>
	``

Video attributes

The HTML5 video and audio elements can use various attributes to control the appearance and various functionality of the control

Attribute	Value	Description
autoplay	{boolean}	Video plays automatically
controls	{boolean}	Video controls displayed
height	{number} pixels	Height of the video player
loop	{boolean}	Video plays unlimited loop
preload	{boolean}	Video loaded at page load and ready to play
poster	{URL}	URL of an image to show until the user plays or seeks
src	{URL}	URL of the video
width	{number} pixels	Width of the video player

Audio Attributes

Attribute	Value	Description
autoplay	{boolean}	Audio will start playing automatically
controls	{boolean}	Displays Audio controls
preload	{boolean}	Audio will preload at page load, and be ready to play. This attribute will be ignored if *autoplay* is present.
src	{URL}	URL of the audio to play

Handling media playback and load state

Various events specify conditions when event was generated

Event	Description
abort	Playback is aborted
canplay	Media is available for playback
ended	Playback completed
error	Error occurred
loadeddata	First frame of the media has loaded
loadstart	Media loading begins
pause	Playback pause
play	Playback start
progress	Notification of the media download progress
ratechange	Playback speed change
seeked	Seek operation completion
seeking	Seek operation start
suspend	Media loading suspended
volumechange	Audio volume change
waiting	Requested event is delayed pending the completion of another event

Web Workers (WW)

JavaScript was designed to run in a single-threaded environment, meaning multiple scripts cannot run at the same time causing browser to crash in a CPU intensive environment. Web Workers allow browser to perform individual tasks on in the background without interfering with other scripts. While the worker is running, user can continue using web browser without waiting for processes to complete.

- WW run in an isolated memory thread. WW are relatively processor-intensive background scripts not intended to be overused since they can consume CPU and slow down or crash the system.
- Creating a new worker involves calling **Worker()** constructor in the parent HTML file, defining a URL to an external JavaScript script based worker to execute it in the thread, and setting that worker's **onmessage** property to an appropriate event handler function in order to receive notifications from the worker.
- The JavaScript code sets event listeners and communicates with the script that spawned it from the main page: **var worker = new Worker('runWorker.js')**. The browser then will spawn a new worker thread, which is downloaded asynchronously. If the path to the worker returns an 404 error, the worker will fail silently.
- WW can import multiple JavaScript files **importScripts('worker1.js', 'worker2.js')**.
- Workers are capable to spawn child workers, the *subworkers*, which must be hosted within the same origin as the parent page.

The next topic is a basic example of WW tandem: a parent HTML and child worker file.

Parent HTML file

Description	Code
Head and body	`<!DOCTYPE HTML>` `<html><head><title></title></head><body>`
Defines a container to display the output	`<p>Message:` `<output id=field style=color:blue><output></p>`
WW is initialized with the URL of a JavaScript file	`<script>` `var worker = new Worker('WebWorker.js');`

The data is passed to the worker via the **postMessage()** method	`worker.onmessage = function(event) {`
	`document.getElementById('field').textContent =`
	`event.data;alert("WebWorker says: " + event.data);}`

onerror event can be used to log errors	`worker.onerror = function (event) {`
	`console.log(event.message, event);}`
	`worker.postMessage('22.95');`
	`</script><body></html>`

WebWorker.js code

Description	Code
■ Message received using the **onmessage** event ■ The data is passed back to the web page by using **postMessage()** method	```onmessage = function(event) {

var message = "The current price is $" + event.data;

postMessage(message);}``` |

- Web Workers can be stopped by calling **worker.terminate()** method from the main page, or by calling **self.close()** inside of the worker itself.

- Due to the multi-threaded nature, WW can only access a limited set of JavaScript's features:

  - Objects: **navigator**, **location** (read-only), **XMLHttpRequest**

  - Methods: **setTimeout()**, **clearTimeout()**, **setInterval()**, **clearInterval()**, **importScripts()**

  - Application Cache

  - Spawning other web workers

- Workers do NOT have access to: the DOM and objects: **window**, **document**, **parent**

- Inline Workers can be created without having to a separate worker utilizing the *BlobBuilder* interface, and appending the worker code as a string

- Unlike other browsers, Google Chrome has security restrictions to WW local access

Web Sockets

Web Sockets is a bidirectional full-duplex communication technology which operates over a single socket. Web Sockets provides simple alternative to AJAX utilizing **send()** method to send data and the **onmessage** event handler to receive data from server to browser.

- This API creates a *WebSocket* object **var Socket = new WebSocket(url, [protocal]);**
- The **URL** argument, defines the target connection URL.
- The **protocal** attribute is optional, and if present, specifies a sub-protocol that the server must support for the connection to be successful.

Following are the methods, attributes, and events, associated with WebSocket object.

WebSocket methods

Method	Description
Socket.send()	Transmits data using the connection
Socket.close()	Terminates any existing connection

WebSocket attributes

Attribute	Description
Socket.readyState	The read-only attribute **readyState** defines state of the connection. The possible values, were connection... - **0** has not yet been established - **1** is established and communication is possible - **2** is going through the closing handshake - **3** has been closed or could not be opened
Socket.bufferedAmount	The read-only attribute **bufferedAmount** defines the number of bytes of UTF-8 text that have been queued using **send()** method

WebSocket events

Event	Event Handler	Description
open	Socket.onopen	Occurs when socket connection is established
message	Socket.onmessage	Occurs when client receives data from server
error	Socket.onerror	Occurs when client receives data from server
close	Socket.onclose	Occurs when connection is closed

WebSocket example

What's great about the WebSocket API is that server and client can push messages bi-directionally to each other at any given time. Unlike AJAX, WebSocket is not limited to requests made by the client, instead WebSocket servers and clients can push messages to each other. The WebSocket example:

Description	Code

Head and body	```<!DOCTYPE HTML>```
	 ```<html><head><title>code example</title></head><body>```
	
	 ```<script>```

■ Socket instance created	```var socket = new WebSocket('ws://localhost:8080');```
■ Socket opened	```socket.onopen = function(event) {```
■ Message sent	```socket.send('I am the listening client');```
■ Listening messages	```socket.onmessage = function(event) {``` ```console.log('Message received ',event);};```
■ Closed socket notification	```socket.onclose = function(event) {``` ```console.log('Client notified of closed socket',event);};};```
	```</script><body></html>```

Microdata and Semantic Web

The next generation of the World Wide Web will be the Semantic Web, which will significantly improve the level of efficiency with which we use the web. The web will evolve into one ocean of standardized machine-readable semantic *metadata*, one global database of uniformly formatted semantic entities. I will call these entities "semantic objects". Every entity will become a semantic object and every entity will have assigned standardized semantic properties: any product, person, concept, entity, even a single word. For instance, a personal computer will have the properties: type, manufacturer, color, weight, etc. The standardized machine-readable semantic language *RDF* is now in works by The W3 Consortium. The RDF will describe:

- Object semantic properties
- Relationships between semantic objects.

Semantic data will be fetched, analyzed and processed by various web applications, portlets and widgets, also helping us search, shop, sell, market, travel, research, invent, create, communicate, socialize, etc. While the current web is very fragmented, inefficient and redundant, the future semantic web will be unified, efficient, and significantly less redundant.

Of course we can only take advantage of the semantic web when the vast majority of web sites will adopt semantic standards; but in the meantime we can utilize the "Semantic Web Lite", the HTML5 *Microdata* API to embed semantic properties into web pages.

Microdata basics

Microdata API extends HTML by adding custom vocabularies offering a standardized way to embed machine-readable custom semantic properties in HTML document. At a high level, *microdata* is expressed by of a group of name-value pairs which can be nested. The groups are called *items*, and each name-value pair is a *property*. Example:

- The **itemscope** attribute creates an item
- The **itemprop** attribute adds a property to an item
- Two of these items have the same property 'price'
- An element can introduce multiple properties at once, e.g. type, color, operating system:
  <span itemprop="type-desktop color-beige os-winows7">Dell PC</span>

```
<div itemscope>

<p>Bread $<span itemprop=price>
2.50</span>.</p>

</div>

<div itemscope>

<p>Milk $<span itemprop=price>
3.20</span>.</p>

</div>
```

- An element can introduce multiple properties at once, e.g. type, color, operating system:
  <span itemprop="type-desktop color-beige os-winows7">Dell PC</span>
- The global document object will have **getItems()** function for supported browsers:
  function microdataSupport() {return !!document.getItems;}.
- Search engines utilize HTML-based microdata. Browsers, on the other hand, will take advantage of *microdata* DOM API functions.

Global microdata attributes

Global attributes can be used to specify *items*.

Attribute	Description
itemscope	A boolean attribute that creates a group of name-value pairs called an *item*
itemtype	URL which defines an *item* vocabulary name
itemid	Global unique identifier for an *item*
itemprop	Property definition of an *item*
itemref	Non-descendent properties of element with the *itemscope* attribute can be associated with the item via reference to an element ID

Property types

Description	Code
▪ To make *microdata* reusable, it is necessary to define item *type*, which can be identified as namespace URL. ▪ An item can only have one type which gives the context for the properties, consequently defining a *vocabulary*, identified by the **itemtype** attribute and associated with their global identifier utilizing the **itemid** attribute. ▪ Sometimes an item describes a topic that has a global identifier, e.g. Social Security Number. ▪ An item could have multiple properties defined by **itemprop** attribute. This item has three properties.	```<div itemscope itemtype=http://data-vocabulary.org/Person itemid="urn:ssn:348-54-2857" >```
▪ Properties generally have values that are strings	```<p>My name is <span itemprop=name>Sergey</span>.</p>```
▪ Properties can also have URL values	```<img itemprop=image src=portrait.gif>```
▪ Properties can also have date and time values using the **time** element and its **datetime** attribute	```<p>My birthday is:<time itemprop=birthday datetime="1973-08-14">Aug 14th 1973</time> </p>```
	```</div>```

Geolocation

HTML5 *Geolocation* API, supported already by most modern browsers, allows your location to be shared with certain Web sites you visit. JavaScript is used to determine your latitude and longitude. The location can be used to suggest local points of interests, provide instant directions or create targeted advertising. Browsers must not send location information to Web sites without the user's permission.

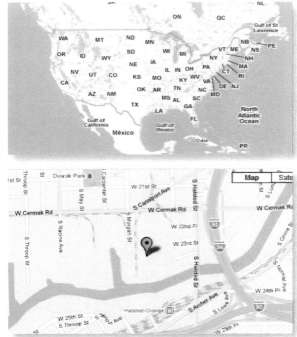

Geolocation API is defined through a **geolocation** child object within the **navigator** object: **navigator.geolocation**

Example of capturing location information

Description	Code

Related HTML markup:
 	
- button
- map
- message placeholder
	`<button id="show_button">Show Position</button>`
	
	`<span id="message"></span>`
	
	`<div id="map"> <img src="http://maps.google.com/maps/api/staticmap?center=35,-90&zoom=2&size=400x250&sensor=true"/></div>`

JavaScript function and variables defined	`<script>`
	
	`(function() { var map = null;`
	
	`var geolog = document.querySelector("#message");`
	
	`var geoMap = document.querySelector("#map");`

Description	Code

■ Latitude and longitude position captured and displayed as map marker	```function showPosition(position) {```
	
	```geolog.textContent = "You're within " + position.coords.accuracy +" meters of (" + position.coords.latitude + ", " + position.coords.longitude + ")";```
	
	```var latLng = new google.maps.LatLng (position.coords.latitude, position.coords.longitude);```
	
	```var marker = new google.maps.Marker ({ position: latLng, map: map });```
	
	```map.setCenter(latLng); map.setZoom(15); }```

	```function handlePositionError(evt) { geolog.textContent = evt.message; }```
	
	```function successPositionHandler(evt) {```
	
	```if (!map) { map = new google.maps.Map (geoMap, { zoom: 3, center: new google.maps. LatLng(35,-90), mapTypeId: google.maps.MapTypeId.ROADMAP }); }```

■ Browser test for geolocation support
 	
■ Geolocation API defined
 	
■ Current Position captured
	```if (navigator.geolocation) { geolog.textContent = 'Checking location...';```
	
	```navigator.geolocation.getCurrentPosition (showPosition, handlePositionError);```
	
	```} else {```
	
	```geolog.textContent='No browser geolocation support'; }}```

■ Google maps API included	```document.querySelector('#show_button'). addEventListener('click', successPositionHandler, false);```
	
	```geoMap.addEventListener ('click', successPositionHandler, false); })();```
	
	```</script>```
	
	```<script src=http://maps.google.com/maps/api/js?sensor=true> </script>```

Four Geolocation API objects

	Object	Description	Usage
1	*geolocation*	Service object that allows widgets to access geographic location	`var geolocation = navigator. geolocation;`

2	*Position*	Specifies the current geographic location	`Position {`
			`    coords : {`
			
			`        latitude : Number,`
			`        longitude : Number,`
			`        altitude : Number,`
			`        accuracy : Number,`
			`        altitudeAccuracy : Number,`
			`        heading : Number,`
			`        speed : Number },`
			
			`    timestamp : Date }`

3	*PositionOptions*	Specifies a set of options for retrieving the geographic location of the device.	`getCurrentPosition` `(callback, ErrorCallback, options)`
4	*PositionError*	runtime error information for geolocation method	`Altitude in meters above the` *World Geodetic System (WGS 84)* `ellipsoid`

1. Geolocation object

Properties enclosed in [ ] are optional. If the optional property value is undefined, it is set to **null**.

Method	Values	
`getCurrentPosition()` `watchPosition()`	Syntax	getCurrentPosition(callback, ErrorCallback, options) watchPosition(callback, ErrorCallback, options)
	Parameters	▪ **callback**: asynchronous callback method that retrieves the location. Type: **function(Position)** ▪ **[ErrorCallback]**: an error processing the asynchronous call with the PositionError object that stores the returned error. Type: **function(PositionError)** ▪ **[options]**: location retrieval options: accuracy, timeout, cached location. Type: **PositionOptions**

Method	Values			
	Error and exception codes	Code	Constant	Description
		0	unknown_error	failed to retrieve the location due to an unknown error
		1	permission_denied	application does not have permission to use the Location Service
		2	position_unavailable	location could not be determined
		3	timeout	failed to retrieve the location within the specified interval
getPositionUsingMethodName()	Syntax	getPositionUsingMethodName (scbCallback, methodName, errCallback)		
	Parameters	■ **scbCallback**: asynchronous callback method that retrieves the location Type: **Function(position, methodName)** ■ **methodName**: positioning system specification: Cellular ID, GPS, AGPS, [**errCallback**]. Type: string ■ [**errCallback**]: called with the **PositionError** object that stores the returned error information Type: **Function(methodName,errObject)**		
	Exception codes	■ MISSING_ARG_ERR: The **methodName** is not supported ■ INVALID_ARG_ERR: service already in use		
	Error codes	■ NOT_SUPPORTED_ERR: a mandatory argument is missing from the method call ■ SERVICE_IN_USE_ERR: the value of a method parameter is not of the expected type		
clearWatch()	Syntax	clearWatch(watchId)		
	Parameters	**watchId**: unique ID of the **watchPosition** call to cancel. Type: number		
	Exception codes	UNKNOWN_ERROR: The invalid **watchId** parameter value, which must be a number.		

2. Position object

The `getCurrentPosition()` and `getPositionUsingMethodName()` methods capture location information asynchronously utilizing an object *Position*. The location value is a set of geographic coordinates, direction and speed. Properties enclosed in [ ] are optional.

Property	Type	Description
coords	objects	Geographic location defined as a set of coordinates, direction & speed
coords.latitude	number	Latitude value range expressed in decimal degrees: -90.00 to +90.00
coords.longitude	number	Longitude value range expressed in decimal degrees: -180.00 to +180.00
[coords.altitude]	number	Altitude in meters above the *World Geodetic System (WGS 84)* ellipsoid
[coords.accuracy]	number	Latitude and longitude accuracy in meters
[coords.altitudeAccuracy]	number	Altitude accuracy in meters
[coords.heading]	number	Movement direction of in degrees counting clockwise relative to true north
[coords.speed]	number	Current ground speed in meters per second
timestamp	date	Time recorded for the location retrieved and the *Position* object created

3. PositionOptions object

The `PositionOptions` object specifies a set of options for the third argument of the `getCurrentPosition()` method:
`getCurrentPosition(callback, ErrorCallback, options)`

Property	Type	Description
enableHighAccuracy	Boolean	Specifies whether the widget wants to receive the most accurate location estimate possible. By default this is false.
timeout	Number	The timeout property is the number of milliseconds your web application is willing to wait for a position.
maximumAge	Number	Specifies the expiry time in milliseconds for cached location information.

Code example: `geolocation.getCurrentPosition (showLocation, errorHandler, { maximumAge: 45000 });`

4. PositionError object

If an error occurs the geolocation methods `getCurrentPosition()` and `watchPosition()` use the error handler callback method **ErrorCallback** which is provided by the **PositionError** object.

The PositionError object properties

Property	Type	Description
code	Number	A numeric error codes (also listed within the geolocation object topic):

Code	Constant	Description
0	unknown_error	failed to retrieve the location due to an unknown error
1	permission_denied	application does not have permission to use the Location Service
2	position_unavailable	location could not be determined
3	timeout	failed to retrieve the location within the specified interval

Property	Type	Description
message	String	Error description

Web Storage

Two types of web storage APIs

Web Storage APIs allow a string client side data storage in a key-value pair database of two types: the *sessionStorage* and the *localStorage*.

- The sessionStorage is similar to HTTP session cookie retaining data only for a single session.

- The localStorage stores data locally across browser sessions and even system reboots.

- The Web Storage API is separate from the *Web SQL Database* API which provides a offline SQL database. As of 10 November 2010, the official working draft indicates that the standardization of Web SQL Database API is blocked due to a lack of different implementations

- Web Storage API have a few advantages over the conventional HTTP session cookie:
  - Cookies are included with every HTTP request, slowing down the web application
  - Cookies send data unencrypted over the internet
  - Cookies are limited to about 4 KB of data

Local vs. Session storage

localStorage	sessionStorage
Value spans multiple windows	Multiple transactions could be performed in different windows simultaneously, since value is visible only within the window of origin
Value lasts beyond the current session	Value exists as long as its window or tab

Setting storage values

This example is applicable to both types of storage: just substitute *localStorage* with *sessionStorage*.

Description	Code

■ Variable declared
■ Storage is set to the initial value
	```(function () {function displayStorageResults () {```
	
	```var StorageValue = localStorage["Zip code"];```
	
	```document.getElementById("storageResults").innerHTML = (StorageValue)?StorageValue: "(empty)"; }```
	
	```displayStorageResults();```

■ The **onclick** event could call the function to update the storage	```document.getElementById("setStorage").onclick = function () {```
	
	```localStorage["Zip code"] = "60611";```
	```displayStorageResults(); };```

■ The **onclick** event could call the function to clear the storage	```document.getElementById("clearStorage").onclick = function () {```
	
	```localStorage.clear();```
	```displayStorageResults(); };```
	
	```})();```

In this example the **textarea** HTML element is utilized to store and retrieve *localStorage* values

■ *setItem(key, value)* method creates a structured clone of the given value

■ *getItem(key)* method retrieves a structured clone of the given value

■ *addEventListener* method receives storage events

```
(function() {  var area = document.querySelector('#a');

if (!area.value) {
area.value = window.localStorage.getItem ('value'); }

updateLog(false);

document.querySelector('#save-a').addEventListener('click',
function () {
window.localStorage.setItem ('value', area.value);
window.localStorage.setItem ('timestamp', (new Date()).
getTime()); updateLog(true); }, false);

function updateLog(new_save) {
var log = document.querySelector("#a-log");
var delta = 0;

    if (window.localStorage.getItem ('value')) {

delta = ((new Date()).getTime() - (new Date()).
setTime(window.localStorage.getItem('timestamp'))) / 1000;

    if (new_save) {  log.textContent = 'Saved!';

setTimeout(function() { log.textContent = ""; }, 2000);

} else { log.textContent = 'last saved:' + delta + 's ago';

}  }  }  })();
```

Storage API properties and methods

Object	Description	
`storage`	description	`storage` object provides access to a list of key/value pairs (items)
	properties	■ `localStorage` Stores data with no time limit ■ `sessionStorage` Stores data for the life of window or tab

Methods applicable to both storage attributes

Methods	Description	
`getItem(key)`	description	Returns a structured clone of the current value associated with the key
	syntax	`sValue = object.getItem(sKey)`
	parameters	sKey: required UTF-16 string, including the empty string
`setItem(key, value)`	description	Creates a structured clone of the given value
	syntax	`object.setItem(sKey, sValue)`
	parameters	■ sKey: required UTF-16 string, including the empty string ■ sValue: required UTF-16 string of the key/value pair
`initStorageEvent()`	description	Initializes the event in a way identical to the similarly-named method in the DOM Events interfaces
	syntax	`StorageEvent.initStorageEvent(eventType, canBubble, canCancel, keyArg, oldValueArg, newValueArg, urlArg, storageAreaArg)`
	parameters	■ eventType: required. The `storage` value, or a custom event ■ canBubble: required parameter specifies if an event should propagate upward. Values: `true` | `false` ■ canCancel: required parameter specifies if the default action can be canceled. Values: `true` | `false` ■ keyArg: required storage key, returned in the key attribute ■ oldValueArg: required previous value of the storage key, or null, returned in the `oldValue` attribute of the event ■ newValueArg: required new value of the storage key, or null, returned in the `newValue` attribute of the event ■ urlArg: required address of the document, returned in the URL attribute of the processing event ■ storageAreaArg: required storage object that is modified, returned in the `storageArea` attribute of the event
`key(lIndex)`	description	Retrieves the key at the specified index in the collection
	syntax	`sKey = object.key(lIndex)`
	parameters	Index: required 0-based index of the list entry, up to the length of the collection

clear()	description	Empties the list associated with the object of all key/value pair
	syntax	`object.clear()`
	example	`<button onclick=localStorage.clear()>` `clear stored values`
removeItem(key)	description	Removes the key/value pair with the given key from the list associated with the object
	syntax	`object.removeItem(sKey)`
	parameters	sKey: required UTF-16 string, including the empty string

Drag and Drop

Drag and Drop (DnD) interface makes it easy to add, reorder and delete items using mouse input. HTML 5 Drag and Drop API delivers native DnD support, introducing new interface objects & attributes.

Simple Drag and Drop example

Description	Code
HTML elements	`<body>`

■ Two draggable **span** elements
■ One target **div** element
	`<span draggable="true" id="object1"`
	`ondragstart="dragit(this, event)" style="background-`
	`color: #B7D882">Drag Object 1</span>`

	`<span draggable="true" id="object2"`
	`ondragstart="dragit(this, event)" style="background-`
	`color: #B8C2D9">Drag Object 2</span>`

	`<div id="target" ondrop="dropit(this,`
	`event)" ondragenter="cancelEvent()"`
	`ondragover="cancelEvent()" style="width:250px;`
	`height:80px; background-color: #00AEEF">Target</div>`

■ JavaScript functions defined	`<script>`
	`function dragit(target, e) {` `e.dataTransfer.setData('Text', target.id);}`

	`function dropit(target, e) {`
	`var drg_id = e.dataTransfer.getData('Text');`
	`target.appendChild(document.getElementById(drg_id));`
	`e.preventDefault();}`

	`function cancelEvent() {window.event.` `returnValue=false;}`
	`</script>`
	`</body>`

DnD interfaces

Interface	Content	
DataTransfer	description	Drag events record drag data in an object called *dataTransfer.* The recorded drag data can be manipulated using object methods and attributes
	methods	■ getData(string type): returns the data ■ setData(string type, string data): sets the data for a given type ■ setDragImage(string type, string data): sets the dragging image

	attributes	■ dataTransfer.*dropEffect* [= value]
		  - returns the kind of operation that is currently selected
		  - changes the selected operation
		  - values: **none, copy, link**, and **move**
		■ dataTransfer.*effectAllowed* [= value]
		  - returns the kinds of operations that are to be allowed
		  - changes the allowed operations
		  - values: **none, copy, copyLink, copyMove, link, linkMove, move, all** and **uninitialized**
		■ dataTransfer.*types*
		  - returns a **DOMStringList**, listing the **dragstart** event formats
		  - if any files are being dragged, then the type will be the string "Files"
		■ dataTransfer.*clearData*([format])
		  - removes the data of the specified formats
		  - removes all data if the argument is omitted
		■ dataTransfer.*setData*(format, data: adds data
		■ data = dataTransfer.*getData*(format):
		  - returns the specified data or an empty string
		■ dataTransfer.*files*: returns a **FileList** of the files being dragged
		■ dataTransfer.*setDragImage*(element, x, y): updates the drag feedback, replacing any previously specified feedback
		■ dataTransfer.*addElement*(element):
		  - adds the element to the list of elements rendering the drag feedback

Interface	Content	
DataTransferItems	description	Each **DataTransfer** object is associated with a **DataTransferItems** object. Attributes can manipulate drag data store entries
	attributes	■ items.length: returns the number of items ■ items[index]: returns the **DataTransferItem** object representing the **indexth** entry ■ delete items[index]: removes the **indexth** entry ■ items.clear( ): removes all the entries ■ items.add(data) items.add(data, type): adds a new entry
DragEvent	description	The drag-and-drop processing model involves several events which utilize the **DragEvent** interface
	events	■ dragstart: initiate the drag-and-drop action ■ dragenter: reject user target selection ■ dragover: reset the drag operation to "none" ■ dragleave: mouse leaves an element while a drag is occurring ■ drag: continue the drag-and-drop action ■ drop: preforms the actual drop ■ dragend: user finishes a drag operation releasing the mouse button
	attributes	■ draggable: values: **true**, **false**, **auto** ■ dropzone: optional, unordered set of unique ASCII case-insensitive space-separated tokens. Values: **copy**, **move**, **link**
UndoManager	description	Manages the *undo object* entries in the undo transaction history
	attributes	■ window.undoManager: returns the **UndoManager** object ■ undoManager.length: number of undo history entries ■ data = undoManager.item(index) undoManager[index]: entry with **index** in the undo history ■ undoManager.position: number of the current entry in the undo history ■ undoManager.add(data, title): adds the entry to the undo history ■ undoManager.remove(index): removes the entry to the undo history ■ undoManager.clearUndo( ): removes all undo history entries ■ undoManager.clearRedo( ): removes all redo history entries
UndoManagerEvent	description	The *UndoManagerEvent* interface and the *undo* and *redo* events
	attributes	■ event.data: data that was passed to the **add( )** method

Other Web Application APIs

Contacts API

Defines an API that provides access to a user's unified address book, where address book data may be sourced from a various online and local sources.

The is basic example of searching address book, obtaining the 'name' and 'emails' properties and filter the list to Contact records:

```
function successContactFindCallback(contacts) {
for (var i in contacts)
alert(contacts[i].displayName); }

function generalErrorCB(error) {
alert(error.code); }

navigator.service.contacts.find(['name',
'emails'], successContactFindCallback,
generalErrorCB,{filter: 'Sergey'});
```

Programmable HTTP Caching and Serving

Defines APIs for off-line serving of requests to HTTP resources using static and dynamic responses, extending the function of application caches defined in HTML5. Example:

- An application captures a resource as part of an atomic cache transaction.
- Once the resource is captured successfully, the application places the captured representation in to service

```
var uri = ...

var cache = window.applicationCache;

//cache and take advantage of the new cache

cache.immediate(uri);
```

- Browser then serves this static representation when an application issues a **GET** request for that resource either through page navigation or an **XMLHttpRequest**

```
var req = new XMLHttpRequest();

req.open('GET', uri);

...

req.send();
```

Media Capture API

The Capture API defines an interface to access the microphone and camera of a hosting device.

Media Capture interfaces

Interface	Type	Metods
DeviceCapture	description	Exposed on the `navigator.device` object
	attributes	`Capture`
Capture	description	Creates a structured clone of the given value
	attributes	■ supportedAudioFormats: array of MediaFileData objects containing audio formats supported by the microphone ■ supportedImageFormats: array of MediaFileData objects containing images formats supported by the hosting device camera ■ supportedVideoFormats: array of MediaFileData objects containing video formats supported by the hosting device camera
	methods	■ captureAudio: launch audio recorder ■ captureImage: launch camera application ■ captureVideo: launch camera application
CaptureCB	methods	■ onSuccess: captured file list
CaptureErrorCB	methods	■ onError: unsuccessful capture
CaptureError	description	Encapsulates all errors in the Capture API
	attributes	■ Code: error code
CaptureImageOptions	description	Image capture operation configuration options
CaptureVideoOptions CaptureAudioOptions	attributes	■ duration: maximum duration of a single clip in seconds. ■ limit: upper limit of clips/images user can record. Value => **1**
PendingOperation	methods	■ cancel: terminate the pending asynchronous operation and close the recording application automatically

This is an example of launching a camera application to retrieve pictures.

```
function success(data) {
var container = document.createElement("div");

  for (var i in data) {

    var img = document.createEle ment("img");
    img.src = data[i].url;
    container.appendChild(img);}

  document.body.appendChild(container);}

function error(err) {

  if (err.code === err.CAPTURE_INTERNAL_ERR) {
alert("The capture failed due to an error.");}

  else { alert("Other error occured.");}}

navigator.device.capture.captureImage(success,
error, { limit: 1 });
```

Browser Compatibility

Web applications

	Desktop					Mobile		
	IE	FireFox	Safari	Chrome	Opera	iOS	Opera	Android
Audio & Video	9	3.5	4	6	10.5	4	✗	2.3
Drag and Drop	6	3.5	4	6	11.1?	✗	✗	2.1
File API	9?	3.6	6	6	11.1?	✗	✗	✗
Geolocation	9?	3.5	5	6	10.6	3.2	✗	2.1*
Inline SVG	9	4	6	7	11.1?	✗	✗	✗
Local Storage	8	3.5	4	6	10.5	3.2	✗	2.1
Offline Apps	9?	3.5	4	6	10.6	3.2	10?	2.1*
postMessage	8	3	4	6	10.5	3.2	10?	2.1
Session History	9?	4	5	6	11.1?	4	✗	2.2
SVG basic	9	3	3.2	6	10.5	3.2	10	✗
SVG Filters	✗	3	6	10*	11.1	✗	10?	✗
SVG Fonts	✗	✗	3.2	6	11.1	3.2	10?	✗
SVG SMIL animation	✗	4	5	6	10.5	3.2*	10	✗
WebGL 3D	9?	4	6*	9	11.1?	✗	✗	✗
WebSockets	9?	4*	5	6	11*	4.2	10?	✗
Web SQL	9?	✗	3.2	6	10.5	3.2	✗	2.1
Web Workers	9?	3.5	4	6	10.6	✗	✗	✗
Overall compliance	**35%**	**87%**	**97%**	**97%**	**64%**	**68%**	**15%**	**41%**

Audio and video codecs

	Chrome	FireFox	Opera	Safari		IE		
audio	9	4	11	5	6	7	8	9
Ogg Vorbis	✓	✓	✓					
mp3	✓			✓				✓
wav	✓	✓	✓	✓				
AACC	✓			✓				✓
video								
Ogg Theora	✓	✓	✓					
H.264	✓			✓				✓
WebM	✓	✓	✓					
MPEG4	✓			✓				

7. Appendix

HTML4 color keywords

Keyword	sRGB value	Keyword	sRGB value
Black	#000000	Green	#008000
Silver	#C0C0C0	Lime	#00FF00
Gray	#808080	Olive	#808000
White	#FFFFFF	Yellow	#FFFF00
Maroon	#800000	Navy	#000080
Red	#FF0000	Blue	#0000FF
Purple	#800080	Teal	#008080
Fuchsia	#FF00FF	Aqua	#00FFFF

X11 color keywords

Color Name	Hex RGB	Decimal	Color Name	Hex RGB	Decimal
AliceBlue	#F0F8FF	240,248,255	BurlyWood	#DEB887	222,184,135
AntiqueWhite	#FAEBD7	250,235,215	CadetBlue	#5F9EA0	95,158,160
Aqua	#00FFFF	0,255,255	Chartreuse	#7FFF00	127,255,0
Aquamarine	#7FFFD4	127,255,212	Chocolate	#D2691E	210,105,30
Azure	#F0FFFF	240,255,255	Coral	#FF7F50	255,127,80
Beige	#F5F5DC	245,245,220	CornflowerBlue	#6495ED	100,149,237
Bisque	#FFE4C4	255,228,196	Cornsilk	#FFF8DC	255,248,220
Black	#000000	0,0,0	Crimson	#DC143C	220,20,60
BlanchedAlmond	#FFEBCD	255,235,205	Cyan	#00FFFF	0,255,255
Blue	#0000FF	0,0,255	DarkBlue	#00008B	0,0,139
BlueViolet	#8A2BE2	138,43,226	DarkCyan	#008B8B	0,139,139
Brown	#A52A2A	165,42,42	DarkGoldenrod	#B8860B	184,134,11

Color Name	Hex RGB	Decimal	Color Name	Hex RGB	Decimal
DarkGray	#A9A9A9	169,169,169	Honeydew	#F0FFF0	240,255,240
DarkGreen	#006400	0,100,0	HotPink	#FF69B4	255,105,180
DarkKhaki	#BDB76B	189,183,107	IndianRed	#CD5C5C	205,92,92
DarkMagenta	#8B008B	139,0,139	Indigo	#4B0082	75,0,130
DarkOliveGreen	#556B2F	85,107,47	Ivory	#FFFFF0	255,255,240
DarkOrange	#FF8C00	255,140,0	Khaki	#F0E68C	240,230,140
DarkOrchid	#9932CC	153,50,204	Lavender	#E6E6FA	230,230,250
DarkRed	#8B0000	139,0,0	LavenderBlush	#FFF0F5	255,240,245
DarkSalmon	#E9967A	233,150,122	LawnGreen	#7CFC00	124,252,0
DarkSeaGreen	#8FBC8F	143,188,143	LemonChiffon	#FFFACD	255,250,205
DarkSlateBlue	#483D8B	72,61,139	LightBlue	#ADD8E6	173,216,230
DarkSlateGray	#2F4F4F	47,79,79	LightCoral	#F08080	240,128,128
DarkTurquoise	#00CED1	0,206,209	LightCyan	#E0FFFF	224,255,255
DarkViolet	#9400D3	148,0,211	LightGoldenrodYellow	#FAFAD2	250,250,210
DeepPink	#FF1493	255,20,147	LightGreen	#90EE90	144,238,144
DeepSkyBlue	#00BFFF	0,191,255	LightGrey	#D3D3D3	211,211,211
DimGray	#696969	105,105,105	LightPink	#FFB6C1	255,182,193
DodgerBlue	#1E90FF	30,144,255	LightSalmon	#FFA07A	255,160,122
FireBrick	#B22222	178,34,34	LightSeaGreen	#20B2AA	32,178,170
FloralWhite	#FFFAF0	255,250,240	LightSkyBlue	#87CEFA	135,206,250
ForestGreen	#228B22	34,139,34	LightSlateGray	#778899	119,136,153
Fuchsia	#FF00FF	255,0,255	LightSteelBlue	#B0C4DE	176,196,222
Gainsboro	#DCDCDC	220,220,220	LightYellow	#FFFFE0	255,255,224
GhostWhite	#F8F8FF	248,248,255	Lime	#00FF00	0,255,0
Gold	#FFD700	255,215,0	LimeGreen	#32CD32	50,205,50
Goldenrod	#DAA520	218,165,32	Linen	#FAF0E6	250,240,230
Gray	#808080	128,128,128	Magenta	#FF00FF	255,0,255
Green	#008000	0,128,0	Maroon	#800000	128,0,0
GreenYellow	#ADFF2F	173,255,47	MediumAquamarine	#66CDAA	102,205,170

Color Name	Hex RGB	Decimal	Color Name	Hex RGB	Decimal
MediumBlue	#0000CD	0,0,205	PowderBlue	#B0E0E6	176,224,230
MediumOrchid	#BA55D3	186,85,211	Purple	#800080	128,0,128
MediumPurple	#9370DB	147,112,219	Red	#FF0000	255,0,0
MediumSeaGreen	#3CB371	60,179,113	RosyBrown	#BC8F8F	188,143,143
MediumSlateBlue	#7B68EE	123,104,238	RoyalBlue	#4169E1	65,105,225
MediumSpringGreen	#00FA9A	0,250,154	SaddleBrown	#8B4513	139,69,19
MediumTurquoise	#48D1CC	72,209,204	Salmon	#FA8072	250,128,114
MediumVioletRed	#C71585	199,21,133	SandyBrown	#F4A460	244,164,96
MidnightBlue	#191970	25,25,112	SeaGreen	#2E8B57	46,139,87
MintCream	#F5FFFA	245,255,250	Seashell	#FFF5EE	255,245,238
MistyRose	#FFE4E1	255,228,225	Sienna	#A0522D	160,82,45
Moccasin	#FFE4B5	255,228,181	Silver	#C0C0C0	192,192,192
NavajoWhite	#FFDEAD	255,222,173	SkyBlue	#87CEEB	135,206,235
Navy	#000080	0,0,128	SlateBlue	#6A5ACD	106,90,205
OldLace	#FDF5E6	253,245,230	SlateGray	#708090	112,128,144
Olive	#808000	128,128,0	Snow	#FFFAFA	255,250,250
OliveDrab	#6B8E23	107,142,35	SpringGreen	#00FF7F	0,255,127
Orange	#FFA500	255,165,0	SteelBlue	#4682B4	70,130,180
OrangeRed	#FF4500	255,69,0	Tan	#D2B48C	210,180,140
Orchid	#DA70D6	218,112,214	Teal	#008080	0,128,128
PaleGoldenrod	#EEE8AA	238,232,170	Thistle	#D8BFD8	216,191,216
PaleGreen	#98FB98	152,251,152	Tomato	#FF6347	255,99,71
PaleTurquoise	#AFEEEE	175,238,238	Turquoise	#40E0D0	64,224,208
PaleVioletRed	#DB7093	219,112,147	Violet	#EE82EE	238,130,238
PapayaWhip	#FFEFD5	255,239,213	Wheat	#F5DEB3	245,222,179
PeachPuff	#FFDAB9	255,218,185	White	#FFFFFF	255,255,255
Peru	#CD853F	205,133,63	WhiteSmoke	#F5F5F5	245,245,245
Pink	#FFC0CB	255,192,203	Yellow	#FFFF00	255,255,0
Plum	#DDA0DD	221,160,221	YellowGreen	#9ACD32	154,205,50

Web color keywords

Black #000000
Maroon #800000
Green #008000
Navy #000080

Silver #C0C0C0
Red #FF0000
Lime #00FF00
Blue #0000FF

Gray #808080
Purple #800080
Olive #808000
Teal #008080

White #FFFFFF
Fuchsia #FF00FF
Yellow #FFFF00
Aqua #00FFFF

HTML predefined colors

FF – 255	77 – 119	
EE – 238	66 – 102	
DD – 221	55 – 85	
CC – 204	44 – 68	
BB – 187	33 – 51	
AA – 170	22 – 34	
99 – 153	11 – 17	
88 – 136	00 – 00	

Hex - Dec Conversion

#000000	#330000	#660000	#990000	#CC0000	#FF0000
#003300	#333300	#663300	#993300	#CC3300	#FF3300
#006600	#336600	#666600	#996600	#CC6600	#FF6600
#009900	#339900	#669900	#999900	#CC9900	#FF9900
#00CC00	#33CC00	#66CC00	#99CC00	#CCCC00	#FFCC00
#00FF00	#33FF00	#66FF00	#99FF00	#CCFF00	#FFFF00
#000033	#330033	#660033	#990033	#CC0033	#FF0033
#003333	#333333	#663333	#993333	#CC3333	#FF3333
#006633	#336633	#666633	#996633	#CC6633	#FF6633
#009933	#339933	#669933	#999933	#CC9933	#FF9933
#00CC33	#33CC33	#66CC33	#99CC33	#CCCC33	#FFCC33
#00FF33	#33FF33	#66FF33	#99FF33	#CCFF33	#FFFF33
#000066	#330066	#660066	#990066	#CC0066	#FF0066
#003366	#333366	#663366	#993366	#CC3366	#FF3366
#006666	#336666	#666666	#996666	#CC6666	#FF6666
#009966	#339966	#669966	#999966	#CC9966	#FF9966
#00CC66	#33CC66	#66CC66	#99CC66	#CCCC66	#FFCC66
#00FF66	#33FF66	#66FF66	#99FF66	#CCFF66	#FFFF66
#000099	#330099	#660099	#990099	#CC0099	#FF0099
#003399	#333399	#663399	#993399	#CC3399	#FF3399
#006699	#336699	#666699	#996699	#CC6699	#FF6699
#009999	#339999	#669999	#999999	#CC9999	#FF9999
#00CC99	#33CC99	#66CC99	#99CC99	#CCCC99	#FFCC99
#00FF99	#33FF99	#66FF99	#99FF99	#CCFF99	#FFFF99
#0000CC	#3300CC	#6600CC	#9900CC	#CC00CC	#FF00CC
#0033CC	#3333CC	#6633CC	#9933CC	#CC33CC	#FF33CC
#0066CC	#3366CC	#6666CC	#9966CC	#CC66CC	#FF66CC
#0099CC	#3399CC	#6699CC	#9999CC	#CC99CC	#FF99CC
#00CCCC	#33CCCC	#66CCCC	#99CCCC	#CCCCCC	#FFCCCC
#00FFCC	#33FFCC	#66FFCC	#99FFCC	#CCFFCC	#FFFFCC
#0000FF	#3300FF	#6600FF	#9900FF	#CC00FF	#FF00FF
#0033FF	#3333FF	#6633FF	#9933FF	#CC33FF	#FF33FF
#0066FF	#3366FF	#6666FF	#9966FF	#CC66FF	#FF66FF
#0099FF	#3399FF	#6699FF	#9999FF	#CC99FF	#FF99FF
#00CCFF	#33CCFF	#66CCFF	#99CCFF	#CCCCFF	#FFCCFF
#00FFFF	#33FFFF	#66FFFF	#99FFFF	#CCFFFF	#FFFFFF

#AA0000	
#BB0000	
#CC0000	
#DD0000	
#EE0000	
#FF0000	
#000011	
#000022	
#000033	
#000044	
#000055	
#000066	
#000077	
#000088	
#000099	
#0000AA	
#0000BB	
#0000CC	
#0000DD	
#0000EE	
#0000FF	
#111100	
#222200	
#333300	
#444400	
#555500	
#666600	
#777700	
#888800	
#999900	
#AAAA00	
#BBBB00	
#CCCC00	
#DDDD00	
#EEEE00	
#FFFF00	

#110000	
#220000	
#330000	
#440000	
#550000	
#660000	
#770000	
#880000	
#990000	
#001100	
#002200	
#003300	
#004400	
#005500	
#006600	
#007700	
#008800	
#009900	
#00AA00	
#00BB00	
#00CC00	
#00DD00	
#00EE00	
#00FF00	
#001111	
#002222	
#003333	
#004444	
#005555	
#006666	
#007777	
#008888	
#009999	
#00AAAA	
#00BBBB	
#00CCCC	
#00DDDD	
#00EEEE	
#00FFFF	

Web safe colors in Hex

HTML special characters

Character	HTML Entity	ISO Latin-1 code	Name or meaning
–	&ndash;	&#8211;	en dash
—	&mdash;	&#8212;	em dash
¡	&iexcl;	&#161;	inverted exclamation
¿	&iquest;	&#191;	inverted question mark
"	&quot;	&#34;	quotation mark
"	&ldquo;	&#8220;	left double curly quote
"	&rdquo;	&#8221;	right double curly quote
'	&lsquo;	&#8216;	left single curly quote
'	&rsquo;	&#8217;	right single curly quote
«	&laquo;	&#171;	guillemets, european-style quotation marks
»	&raquo;	&#187;	
(blank space)			non-breaking space
&	&amp;	&#38;	ampersand
¢	&cent;	&#162;	cent
©	&copy;	&#169;	copyright
÷	&divide;	&#247;	divide
>	&gt;	&#62;	greater than
<	&lt;	&#60;	less than
µ	&micro;	&#181;	micron
·	&middot;	&#183;	middle dot
¶	&para;	&#182;	pilcrow (paragraph sign)
±	&plusmn;	&#177;	plus/minus
€	&euro;	&#8364;	Euro currency
£	&pound;	&#163;	British Pound Sterling
®	&reg;	&#174;	registered
§	&sect;	&#167;	section
™	&trade;	&#153;	trademark
¥	&yen;	&#165;	Japanese Yen

Properties which can be animated

Property Name	Type	Property Name	Type
background-color	color	margin-left	length
background-image	only gradients	margin-right	length
background-position	percentage, length	margin-top	length
border-bottom-color	color	max-height	length, percentage
border-bottom-width	length	max-width	length, percentage
border-color	color	min-height	length, percentage
border-left-color	color	min-width	length, percentage
border-left-width	length	opacity	number
border-right-color	color	outline-color	color
border-right-width	length	outline-offset	integer
border-spacing	length	outline-width	length
border-top-color	color	padding-bottom	length
border-top-width	length	padding-left	length
border-width	length	padding-right	length
bottom	length, percentage	padding-top	length
color	color	right	length, percentage
crop	rectangle	text-indent	length, percentage
font-size	length, percentage	text-shadow	shadow
font-weight	number	top	length, percentage
grid-*	various	vertical-align	keywords, length, %
height	length, percentage	visibility	visibility
left	length, percentage	width	length, percentage
letter-spacing	length	word-spacing	length, percentage
line-height	number, length, %	z-index	integer
margin-bottom	length	zoom	number

Online Resources

Web companion for this book	http://html5.belisso.com/
All W3C standards and Drafts	http://www.w3.org/TR/
HTML5 Reference	http://dev.w3.org/html5/html-author/

Index of Elements	http://www.w3.org/TR/html401/index/elements.html
HTML, CSS, SVG cheat sheet	http://www.w3.org/2009/cheatsheet/
Minify CSS	http://www.minifycss.com/css-compressor/
CSS selector test	http://tools.css3.info/selectors-test/test.html
Your browser HTML5/CSS3 support test	http://www.findmebyip.com
Your browser HTML5 support test	http://html5test.com/
HTML5 cross-browser Polyfills	https://github.com/Modernizr/Modernizr/wiki/HTML5-Cross-browser-Polyfills
CSS3 property tests	http://www.westciv.com/iphonetests/
Check cross-browser compatibility	http://browsershots.org/
W3C HTML validator	http://validator.w3.org/
W3C CSS3 validator	http://jigsaw.w3.org/css-validator/
HTML5 validator	http://html5.validator.nu/

HTML5 and CSS3 desktop applications tools

Name	Description	Platform	Licence
Adobe Dreamweaver CS5 with optional HTML5 pack	HTML5 and CSS3 WYSIWYG editing	Windows, Mac	Commercial
Adobe Flash CS5	Exports to HTML5 Canvas	Windows, Mac	Commercial
Adobe Illustrator CS5 with optional HTML5 pack	Exports to SVG and CSS3	Windows, Mac	Commercial
Apple iAd Producer	HTML5 authoring tool	Mac	Free
Total Validator	(X)HTML5 and accessibility validation	Windows, Mac, Linux	Free (basic)
ActiveState Komodo 6	HTML5 and CSS3 markup editing	Windows, Mac, Linux	Free (basic)
Panic Coda	HTML5 and CSS3 markup editing	Mac	Commercial
TextMate with HTML5 bundle	HTML5 and CSS3 markup editing	Mac	Commercial
The Free HTML Editor 9.4	HTML5 and CSS3 markup editing	Windows	Free
CoffeeCup HTML Editor	HTML5 and CSS3 WYSIWYG editing	Windows	Commercial
CSE HTML Validator 10.0	(X)HTML5 and CSS3 validation	Windows	Commercial
Open Validator 2.7	(X)HTML5 validation	Windows, Mac	Free
Sketsa SVG Editor 6.4	SVG editing	Windows	Commercial
BBEdit 9	HTML5 and CSS3 markup editing	Mac	Commercial
Apatana Studio 3 beta	HTML5 and CSS3 markup editing	Windows, Mac, Linux	Free

Acknowledgements

Spacial thanks to the W3C, WHATWG and other contributors:

Ian 'Hixie' Hickson, Aankhen, Aaron Boodman, Aaron Leventhal, Adam Barth, Adam de Boor, Adam Hepton, Adam Roben, Addison Phillips, Adele Peterson, Adrian Bateman, Adrian Sutton, Agustín Fernández, Ajai Tirumali, Akatsuki Kitamura, Alan Plum, Alastair Campbell, Alejandro G. Castro, Alex Bishop, Alex Nicolaou, Alex Rousskov, Alexander J. Vincent, Alexey Feldgendler, Алексей Проскуряков (Alexey Proskuryakov), Alexis Deveria, Allan Clements, Amos Jeffries, Anders Carlsson, Andreas, Andreas Kling, Andrei Popescu, André E. Veltstra, Andrew Clover, Andrew Gove, Andrew Grieve, Andrew Oakley, Andrew Sidwell, Andrew Smith, Andrew W. Hagen, Andrey V. Lukyanov, Andy Heydon, Andy Palay, Anne van Kesteren, Anthony Boyd, Anthony Bryan, Anthony Hickson, Anthony Ricaud, Antti Koivisto, Arne Thomassen, Aron Spohr, Arphen Lin, Aryeh Gregor, Asbjørn Ulsberg, Ashley Sheridan, Atsushi Takayama, Aurelien Levy, Ave Wrigley, Ben Boyle, Ben Godfrey, Ben Lerner, Ben Leslie, Ben Meadowcroft, Ben Millard, Benjamin Carl Wiley Sittler, Benjamin Hawkes-Lewis, Bert Bos, Bijan Parsia, Bil Corry, Bill Mason, Bill McCoy, Billy Wong, Bjartur Thorlacius, Björn Höhrmann, Blake Frantz, Boris Zbarsky, Brad Fults, Brad Neuberg, Brad Spencer, Brady Eidson, Brendan Eich, Brenton Simpson, Brett Wilson, Brett Zamir, Brian Campbell, Brian Korver, Brian Kuhn, Brian Ryner, Brian Smith, Brian Wilson, Bryan Sullivan, Bruce D'Arcus, Bruce Lawson, Bruce Miller, C. Williams, Cameron McCormack, Cao Yipeng, Carlos Gabriel Cardona, Carlos Perelló Marín, Chao Cai, Channy Yun, Charl van Niekerk, Charles Iliya Krempeaux, Charles McCathieNevile, Chris Apers, Chris Cressman, Chris Evans, Chris Morris, Chris Pearce, Christian Biesinger, Christian Johansen, Christian Schmidt, Christoph Plenio, Christopher Aillon, Chriswa, Clark Buehler, Cole Robison, Colin Fine, Collin Jackson, Corprew Reed, Craig Cockburn, Csaba Gabor, Csaba Marton, Cynthia Shelly, Daniel Barclay, Daniel Bratell, Daniel Brooks, Daniel Brumbaugh Keeney, Daniel Cheng, Daniel Davis, Daniel Glazman, Daniel Peng, Daniel Schattenkirchner, Daniel Spång, Daniel Steinberg, Danny Sullivan, Darin Adler, Darin Fisher, Darxus, Dave Camp, Dave Hodder, Dave Lampton, Dave Singer, Dave Townsend, David Baron, David Bloom, David Bruant, David Carlisle, David E. Cleary, David Egan Evans, David Flanagan, David Gerard, David Håsäther, David Hyatt, David I. Lehn, David John Burrowes, David Matja, David Remahl, David Smith, David Woolley, DeWitt Clinton, Dean Edridge, Dean Edwards, Debi Orton, Derek Featherstone, Devdatta, Dimitri Glazkov, Dimitry Golubovsky, Dirk Pranke, Divya Manian, Dmitry Titov, dolphinling, Dominique Hazaël-Massieux, Don Brutzman, Doron Rosenberg, Doug Kramer, Doug Simpkinson, Drew Wilson, Edmund Lai, Eduard Pascual, Eduardo Vela, Edward O'Connor, Edward Welbourne, Edward Z. Yang, Eira Monstad, Eitan Adler, Eliot Graff, Elizabeth Castro, Elliott Sprehn, Elliotte Harold, Eric Carlson, Eric Law, Eric Rescorla, Eric Semling, Erik Arvidsson, Erik Rose, Evan Martin, Evan Prodromou, Evert, fantasai, Felix Sasaki, Francesco Schwarz, Francis Brosnan Blazquez, Franck 'Shift' Quélain, Frank Barchard, Fumitoshi Ukai, Futomi Hatano, Gavin Carothers, Gareth Rees, Garrett Smith, Geoffrey Garen, Geoffrey Sneddon, George Lund, Gianmarco Armellin, Giovanni Campagna, Graham Klyne, Greg Botten, Greg Houston, Greg Wilkins, Gregg Tavares, Gregory J. Rosmaita, Grey, Gytis Jakutonis, Håkon Wium Lie, Hallvord Reiar Michaelsen Steen, Hans S. Tømmerhalt, Hans Stimer, Henri Sivonen, Henrik Lied, Henry Mason, Hugh Winkler, Ian Bicking, Ian Davis, Ignacio Javier, Ivan Enderlin, Ivo Emanuel Gonçalves, J. King, Jacques Distler, James Craig, James Graham, James Justin Harrell, James M Snell, James Perrett, James Robinson, Jamie Lokier, Jan-Klaas Kollhof, Jason Kersey, Jason Lustig, Jason White, Jasper Bryant-Greene, Jatinder Mann, Jed Hartman, Jeff Balogh, Jeff Cutsinger, Jeff Schiller, Jeff Walden, Jeffrey Zeldman, Jennifer Braithwaite, Jens Bannmann, Jens Fendler, Jens Lindström, Jens Meiert, Jeremy Keith, Jeremy Orlow, Jeroen van der Meer, Jian Li, Jim Jewett, Jim Ley, Jim Meehan, Jjgod Jiang, João Eiras, Joe Clark, Joe Gregorio, Joel Spolsky, Johan Herland, John Boyer, John Bussjaeger, John Carpenter, John Fallows, John Foliot, John Harding, John Keiser, John Snyders, John-

Mark Bell, Johnny Stenback, Jon Ferraiolo, Jon Gibbins, Jon Perlow, Jonas Sicking, Jonathan Cook, Jonathan Rees, Jonathan Worent, Jonny Axelsson, Jorgen Horstink, Jorunn Danielsen Newth, Joseph Kesselman, Joseph Pecoraro, Josh Aas, Josh Levenberg, Joshua Randall, Jukka K. Korpela, Jules Clément-Ripoche, Julian Reschke, Jürgen Jeka, Justin Lebar, Justin Sinclair, Kai Hendry, Kartikaya Gupta, Kathy Walton, Kelly Norton, Kevin Benson, Kornél Pál, Kornel Lesinski, Kristof Zelechovski, Krzysztof Maczyński, Kurosawa Takeshi, Kyle Hofmann, Léonard Bouchet, Lachlan Hunt, Larry Masinter, Larry Page, Lars Gunther, Lars Solberg, Laura Carlson, Laura Granka, Laura L. Carlson, Laura Wisewell, Laurens Holst, Lee Kowalkowski, Leif Halvard Silli, Lenny Domnitser, Leons Petrazickis, Lobotom Dysmon, Logan, Loune, Luke Kenneth Casson Leighton, Maciej Stachowiak, Magnus Kristiansen, Maik Merten, Malcolm Rowe, Mark Birbeck, Mark Miller, Mark Nottingham, Mark Pilgrim, Mark Rowe, Mark Schenk, Mark Wilton-Jones, Martijn Wargers, Martin Atkins, Martin Dürst, Martin Honnen, Martin Kutschker, Martin Nilsson, Martin Thomson, Masataka Yakura, Mathieu Henri, Matias Larsson, Matt Schmidt, Matt Wright, Matthew Gregan, Matthew Mastracci, Matthew Raymond, Matthew Thomas, Mattias Waldau, Max Romantschuk, Menno van Slooten, Micah Dubinko, Michael Engelhardt, Michael 'Ratt' Iannarelli, Michael A. Nachbaur, Michael A. Puls II, Michael Carter, Michael Daskalov, Michael Enright, Michael Gratton, Michael Nordman, Michael Powers, Michael Rakowski, Michael(tm) Smith, Michal Zalewski, Michel Fortin, Michelangelo De Simone, Michiel van der Blonk, Mihai Şucan, Mihai Parparita, Mike Brown, Mike Dierken, Mike Dixon, Mike Schinkel, Mike Shaver, Mikko Rantalainen, Mohamed Zergaoui, Mounir Lamouri, Ms2ger, NARUSE Yui, Neil Deakin, Neil Rashbrook, Neil Soiffer, Nicholas Shanks, Nicholas Stimpson, Nicholas Zakas, Nickolay Ponomarev, Nicolas Gallagher, Noah Mendelsohn, Noah Slater, NoozNooz42, Ojan Vafai, Olaf Hoffmann, Olav Junker Kjær, Oldřich Vetešník, Oli Studholme, Oliver Hunt, Oliver Rigby, Olivier Gendrin, Olli Pettay, Patrick H. Lauke, Paul Norman, Per-Erik Brodin, Perry Smith, Peter Karlsson, Peter Kasting, Peter Stark, Peter-Paul Koch, Phil Pickering, Philip Jägenstedt, Philip Taylor, Philip TAYLOR, Prateek Rungta, Pravir Gupta, Rachid Finge, Rajas Moonka, Ralf Stoltze, Ralph Giles, Raphael Champeimont, Remco, Remy Sharp, Rene Saarsoo, Rene Stach, Ric Hardacre, Rich Doughty, Richard Ishida, Richard Williamson, Rigo Wenning, Rikkert Koppes, Rimantas Liubertas, Riona Macnamara, Rob Ennals, Rob Jellinghaus, Robert Blaut, Robert Collins, Robert Nyman, Robert O'Callahan, Robert Sayre, Robin Berjon, Rodger Combs, Roland Steiner, Roman Ivanov, Roy Fielding, Ryan King, S. Mike Dierken, Salvatore Loreto, Sam Dutton, Sam Kuper, Sam Ruby, Sam Weinig, Sander van Lambalgen, Sarven Capadisli, Scott González, Scott Hess, Sean Fraser, Sean Hayes, Sean Hogan, Sean Knapp, Sebastian Markbåge, Sebastian Schnitzenbaumer, Seth Call, Shanti Rao, Shaun Inman, Shiki Okasaka, Sierk Bornemann, Sigbjørn Vik, Silvia Pfeiffer, Simon Montagu, Simon Pieters, Simon Spiegel, skeww, Stanton McCandlish, Stefan Haustein, Stefan Santesson, Steffen Meschkat, Stephen Ma, Steve Faulkner, Steve Runyon, Steven Bennett, Steven Garrity, Steven Tate, Stewart Brodie, Stuart Ballard, Stuart Parmenter, Subramanian Peruvemba, Sunava Dutta, Susan Borgrink, Susan Lesch, Sylvain Pasche, T. J. Crowder, Tab Atkins, Tantek Çelik, TAMURA Kent, Ted Mielczarek, Terrence Wood, Thomas Broyer, Thomas Koetter, Thomas O'Connor, Tim Altman, Tim Johansson, Toby Inkster, Todd Moody, Tom Pike, Tommy Thorsen, Travis Leithead, Tyler Close, Vladimir Katardjiev, Vladimir Vukićević, voracity, Wakaba, Wayne Carr, Wayne Pollock, Wellington Fernando de Macedo, Weston Ruter, Will Levine, William Swanson, Wladimir Palant, Wojciech Mach, Wolfram Kriesing, Yang Chen, Ye-Kui Wang, Yehuda Katz, Yi-An Huang, Yngve Nysaeter Pettersen, Yuzo Fujishima, Zhenbin Xu, Zoltan Herczeg, and Øistein E. Andersen.

8. Index

Made in the USA
Lexington, KY
27 June 2011